D1420362

OLDER AND WISER

OLDER AND WISER

New Ideas for Youth Mentoring in the 21st Century

Jean E. Rhodes

HARVARD UNIVERSITY PRESS

Cambridge, Massachusetts, and London, England

2020

Library of Congress Cataloging-in-Publication Data

Title: Older and wiser : new ideas for youth mentoring in the 21st century /
Jean E. Rhodes.
Description: Cambridge, Massachusetts : Harvard University Press, 2020. |
Includes index.
Identifiers: LCCN 2020010124 | ISBN 9780674248076 (cloth)
Subjects: LCSH: Mentoring. | Youth development. | Youth—Psychology. |
Youth—Counseling of.
Classification: LCC BF637.M45 O53 2020 | DDC 158.3—dc23
LC record available at https://lccn.loc.gov/2020010124

In memory of George Albee

Contents

Preface   ix

Introduction   1

1. "The Kind of Justice Which Only a
   Brother Can Give"   9
2. Mentoring by the Numbers   25
3. How Did We Get It So Wrong for So Long?   43
4. Giving Psychology Away   71
5. Specialized Mentoring   87
6. The Promise of Embedded and Blended Mentoring   97
7. The Good Enough Mentor   110
8. The Road to Rigor   122
9. Why We Can't Leave Natural Mentoring to Chance   129
10. The Future of Mentoring   144

Epilogue   148

Notes   153
Acknowledgments   205
Index   207

Preface

I bid farewell to my dad on a brisk November morning in 1978, hugging him one last time before climbing onto my moped and speeding down the driveway. It seemed strange to be arriving at my high school so early on a Saturday, but I was joined by other seniors who were taking their college admissions test in the small town of Allendale, New Jersey. By the time I returned home, my dad was gone, leaving behind thirty years of marriage, four kids, and a complicated legal and financial history. I could not fully comprehend the FBI investigation that forced his departure—any more than I could have fathomed the fact that my classmate Jim Comey would eventually lead that agency. I remember feeling a deep sense of shame and embarrassment. I was also reeling from a recent discovery that my dad had "shortened" his name from Rosensweig to Rhodes, a fairly common response to the anti-Semitism of the 1950s. So, as he left us to assume yet another identity, I felt groundless. I remember very little about the days and weeks that followed his departure, except that I was tanking academically and had no clue about college applications or plans for after high school.

During that difficult period, I personally experienced the benefits of natural mentors, intergenerational relationships forged organically (as opposed to those arranged through formal mentoring programs). One morning, my beloved guidance counselor, Miss Blanchard, a short, sturdy woman with a thick white helmet of hair and the warmest smile imaginable, summoned me out of class. "Jeannie," she said, as I entered her office. "I heard you bought yourself a moped. Mind if I take it for a spin?" In that moment, I felt a welcome relief from my anxiety. When I think about the countless ways that Miss Blanchard looked out for me that year, I feel the deepest sense of gratitude. She must have sensed my potential and, more importantly, how much I needed her. In the weeks that followed, she generously helped me through the college application process. She may have even pulled some strings to get me into college. After all, she called me into her office to triumphantly announce my acceptance to the University of Vermont weeks before I received the official word.

And, had I not attended the University of Vermont, I would never have met the next mentor who changed my life. As a freshman, I had the blind luck of enrolling in an introductory psychology course taught by the pioneering community psychologist George Albee. It did not strike me as the least bit unusual that a world-renowned psychologist and the former president of the American Psychological Association would teach an introductory course. Nor did I have the context to appreciate that Albee's take on modern psychology was a radical departure from what was being taught in most classes across the country. Indeed, my first exposure to psychopathology was through the lens of social inequality, illuminating the pernicious effects of racism, sexism, homophobia, and poverty on mental health. Lectures on the Diagnostic and Statistical Manual (DSM) of the American Psychiatric Association centered on its unreliability and its intractable links with the economic interests of insurance companies. From Albee's vantage point, prevention and empowerment—through political and social change—offered the only real pathway to reducing the incidence of psychopathology. And his course's mantra—"that no mass disorder afflicting human-kind has ever been treated out of existence"—rang from that lecture hall with a force that propelled his students toward careers in public health, social policy, and community psychology. Albee became my first mentor in psychology. I took every course he had to offer and anticipated his annual Vermont Conference on the Primary Prevention of Psychopathology with the devotion of a Harry Potter fan. Albee saw potential in me, and, over time, that changed me. My sense of self shifted from a Jersey girl with an uncertain identity and modest ambition to someone who could and should try to make a difference in the world. As an entering freshman, I had been surprised to learn that there existed nonmedical "doctors." I had never even heard of a PhD, much less met anyone who held such a degree. Within a few short years, I was pursuing one.

My positive experience of being mentored by Albee, in turn, primed me for later mentors, including a much older and wiser psychotherapist who supported me during what could now be considered my own torturous #metoo moment. As a twenty-eight-year-old assistant professor at the University of Illinois Champaign-Urbana, I had taken the bold and professionally suicidal move of backing the sexual misconduct accusations that had been lodged by a graduate student against my senior colleague. With a sense of fear in the pit in my stomach, I described to a roomful of senior faculty members how that male senior colleague had tried to enter my conference hotel room just months earlier while I was on the academic job market. As my credibility came under attack, this mother-earth therapist kept me on firm ground. Another mentor, the prominent social psychologist Joseph McGrath, reached out during those tenuous years, tamping my incipient imposter syndrome and generously offering detailed and always encouraging critiques of my early work.

I feel a mix of relief and fear when I imagine the young person I was back then and how differently things might have turned out in the absence of these natural mentors. As our lives progress, different natural mentors fill different roles until eventually we become the mentors, dispensing our own brand of hard-earned wisdom. But, as my own story illustrates, we cannot prescribe who our mentors will be. Beacons like Miss Blanchard, George Albee, my wise therapist, and Joe McGrath, who step in at just the right moment with just the right help, can make a world of difference. Each mentorship is bound in its own way by a sense of shared purpose, and an alchemy of luck, timing, and connection.

Given the idiosyncratic, purpose-driven nature of natural mentoring, it is little wonder that formal mentoring programs, many of which task strangers with forging friendships essentially stripped of intentionality, have struggled to reproduce such bonds. But, of course, it was never reasonable to believe that formal mentoring programs should resemble those organic relationships. This myth burdened volunteers with unrealistic expectations while stalling the field's alignment with broader scientific communities. Paradoxically, the harder the field pushed to emulate natural mentors, the more it may have weakened the enterprise. The idea that volunteers should be able to routinely deliver transformative ties placed unrealistic pressure on ordinary matches, zapping them of shared purpose and direction, and subverting the delicate balance between finding intimacy and achieving goals. Until the cherished myths, the expectations of deep, transformative bonds, and the disconcerting findings that have emerged from decades of evaluations of formal mentoring programs are somehow reconciled, it will be difficult to muster the will to make the necessary correctives. A deeper appreciation of the field's unique history, as well as data on its modest effectiveness, will enable us to break from the mold and more fully capitalize on all that prevention and intervention science has to offer.

As you read through this sometimes sobering, yet ultimately optimistic, analysis of youth mentoring, bear in mind that I am as invested as anyone in getting it right. In fact, I have been chipping away at researching the mentoring field for more than half my life and, like a compulsive gold miner, just can't seem to stop. Believe me, I've tried. But inevitably, other topics lose their appeal and I find myself returning to research that same rich intellectual seam, hoping to unearth and examine just one more nugget. Over time, some of my views on mentoring have changed, and, now, after thirty years, a broader perspective has emerged, one in which each new finding fits more logically into the broader landscape. I lament that it took so long to gain this current perspective but am confident that some of my hard-earned lessons will offer new solutions to the field.

OLDER AND WISER

For the great enemy of the truth is very often not the lie—
deliberate, contrived and dishonest—but the myth—
persistent, persuasive, and unrealistic.

—JOHN F. KENNEDY

INTRODUCTION

Shawn was just fourteen years old when he had his first police encounter. It was a rainy October afternoon, so he and his friends decided to take brief refuge under a bus shelter as they headed up Washington Avenue in Boston's Dorchester neighborhood. Shawn's gray hoodie was drawn around his cheeks tightly, a strategy he had recently adopted to hide his embarrassing acne flare-ups. Maybe it was the hoodie, maybe it was simply the sight of four black boys messing around in a bus shelter, but it was enough to prompt a patrolling officer to pull up in his squad car and subject the ninth-graders to harsh questioning. As the other boys obliged, answering "yes, sir" and "no, sir," Shawn could feel a familiar wave of anger wash over him. When asked to remove his hood, he bolted, only to be apprehended a few blocks away. Shawn can still recall the sensation of his inflamed cheek pressed against the wet sidewalk.

For years, Shawn's mom had implored him to "stop and think" before lashing out or defying authority figures. But a childhood of traumatic stressors, including the violent arrest of his father and a deadly shooting by gang members in his neighborhood, had put his young brain into near-perpetual fight-or-flight mode. Although his mom had devoted herself to raising Shawn and his younger brother to be safe and resilient, her difficult circumstances and unpredictable work hours had limited her capacity to engage in the sort of "concerted cultivation" of her children that characterized families in affluent suburban communities just a few miles north.[1] Instead, much of her parenting time was spent trying to resolve Shawn's growing behavioral and academic problems.

Noting Shawn's impulsivity, his high school counselor recommended an evaluation for possible attention deficit and hyperactivity disorder (ADHD). But, wary of stigma and medical overreach, his mom opted instead for herbal remedies and a referral for a "positive role model" through a local youth mentoring program. Two months into his freshman year of high school, Shawn began having weekly outings with his mentor, David, a twenty-one-year-old premed student from Boston's Northeastern University.

In many ways, David was the quintessential American volunteer mentor—white, young, educated, and well-intentioned. Most volunteer mentors in the United States are white (65 percent), while roughly the same proportion (60 percent) of mentees are nonwhite. Nearly 40 percent of the children in formal mentoring programs are black.[2] Additionally, David was volunteering in a typical program—one that tasks its volunteers with forging close, one-on-one relationships through conversations and activities.[3] In a recent study, researchers sampled nearly two thousand mentors from thirty programs, selected to represent a wide range of mentoring approaches across nationally representative geographic regions, program types, and youth served.[4] When asked how they spent time with their mentees, mentors' most commonly reported activity was "making time to have fun," followed by discussing important personal issues, going to cultural or other special events, and engaging in creative activities.[5] David explained that, over the course of their five-month relationship, his main goal had been to get to know Shawn and to "be there for him." Over pizza, video games, and football tosses, the two had established a comfortable, if tenuous, bond. David was wary of pushing Shawn away, and lacking any specialized training in working with at-risk youth, he skirted tough topics, including Shawn's recent police encounter.

Youth mentoring programs can vary widely, but most seek to create caring relationships between young people (or mentees) and more experienced nonparental adults (mentors). Shawn's mentoring program was based on the assumption that establishing a close mentor-mentee connection through conversations and fun activities can promote a broad, nonspecific range of positive outcomes while preventing the progression of negative outcomes. This so-called friendship or nonspecific approach, in which the quality of the mentor-mentee relationship is assumed to be the active ingredient, has remained essentially unchanged since the early 1900s.[6] This nonspecific approach grew into Big Brothers Big Sisters, the largest donor- and volunteer-supported mentoring program in the world. Big Brothers Big Sisters now operates in all fifty US states as well as a dozen other countries, including Australia, Canada, New Zealand, Russia, and South Korea. Although Big Brothers Big Sisters and many similar programs can sometimes make a difference, there is growing evidence that more scientific approaches, which directly target the specific needs and circumstances of the youth they serve, are more effective.[7]

Anthony, a fifteen-year-old black high school student from a low-income Chicago neighborhood, was enrolled in a program that exemplifies this newer, more targeted approach. Like Shawn, Anthony was matched with a mentor during the fall of his freshman year. Like Shawn, Anthony lived with his low-income, single mother, was estranged from his father, and sometimes struggled to control his emotions. Anthony had also suffered the effects of exposure to far too many stressors, including what psychologists call "adverse childhood experiences." In fact, his life read like a checklist of such experiences. His family faced severe economic hardship. He lived with his mom, who suffered from bouts of anxiety and depression, and an uncle, who had served time in jail. Anthony had also been a victim of violence in his own neighborhood. Black youth such as Anthony are more likely than other American youth to have adverse childhood experiences; 61 percent of American black youth face at least one.[8]

Anthony's guidance counselor referred him to a youth mentoring program that specializes in boys showing early signs of emotional and behavioral difficulties that put them at risk for gang involvement and dropping out of school. Mentoring programs like Anthony's typically rely on an initial assessment of a youth's needs, strengths, and circumstances and then draw on cognitive-behavioral therapy and related techniques (such as cognitive restructuring, applied relaxation, self-compassion, and / or mindfulness) that target the circumstances and processes (such as maladaptive thoughts, behaviors, and feelings) that can progress into more serious outcomes.[9] Anthony was matched with Jason, a thirty-six-year-old mixed-race professional who was warm and patient, but also eager to get things done. Jason built a friendly rapport with Anthony but, unlike David, Jason viewed relationship building as a necessary stepping-stone for the primary task at hand: skills development. Anthony's program consisted of weekly group sessions that met over the course of two school years and incorporated exercises designed to help mentees identify and label their emotions and learn to react differently to stressors. Over time, Anthony learned to de-escalate emotional arousal through deep breathing exercises and deliberation. Although Anthony initially found these skills to be hard to grasp, Jason helped by role-playing and working with Anthony to apply these skills to his everyday tense encounters.[10]

In the last two decades, formal programs like those serving Shawn and Anthony have multiplied and diversified. There are now over five thousand youth mentoring programs across the United States and a growing global mentoring movement, which together place millions of caring volunteers into one-on-one and group relationships, often with vulnerable youth, each year.[11] Mentoring enjoys strong, bipartisan support, making it one of the few concepts these days on which nearly everyone seems to agree.[12] Yet within the field, there is an ongoing debate over the merits of nonspecific, friendship models versus those that combine the relationship with targeted evidence-based strategies and techniques. There also remains considerable misunderstanding about the scope and effectiveness of youth mentoring programs.

In this book I describe how we've gotten to where we are by assessing the state of youth mentoring programs in the United States and beyond. Chapter 1 provides a broad overview of the political and social forces that have shaped how programs have been structured and construed. I then present more than twenty-five years of studies in Chapter 2, evaluating these programs and tracing the overarching patterns that characterize the field. Overall, youth mentoring programs are not nearly as effective as most people assume, particularly when compared to other interventions with youth. Findings from large-scale randomized control trials, meta-analyses, and recent cost-benefit studies present a disappointing bottom line, with relatively weak effects that have not budged in decades. In Chapter 3, I discuss the assumptions and unique history that brought the mentoring field to this point, and detail new developments that position the field for an explosion of innovation.

I then turn to specific strategies for making youth mentoring more effective. As I argue in Chapter 4, there are compelling data to suggest that well-trained paraprofessionals, including volunteer mentors, can be just as effective as highly trained professionals in targeting and addressing many of the mental health and other challenges facing youth. In Chapter 5, I describe *specialized* mentoring program models, which often deploy carefully trained and supervised mentors to target specific populations and/or outcomes. Many of these programs draw on both cognitive strategies (e.g., self-talk, distraction, and mindfulness) and behavioral strategies (e.g., problem solving, activation, self-monitoring, and relaxation). Specialized models take a targeted mentoring approach and contrast with nonspecific mentoring approaches that emphasize factors that are common to all approaches, such as the quality and intensity of the mentoring bond, mentor and youth motivations, and commitment. Although it is generally the case that specialized programs produce more impressive findings, large, nonspecific programs like Big Brothers Big Sisters struggle to target the widely varied needs of the youth they serve. Moreover, asking the typically uncompensated volunteer in such programs to shoulder the burden of delivering a potentially complicated targeted, evidence-based intervention is as precarious as it is unrealistic. Given these constraints, in Chapter 6, I make the case for two different approaches—*embedded* and *blended* models—in which larger programs train and supervise their mentors to support (but not deliver) evidence-based interventions in ways that help mentees remain engaged and master new skills. In embedded mentoring models, programs dispatch trained volunteers to work within broader systems of care (e.g., schools, child protection services, and juvenile courts), where they can reinforce classroom learning or help support and monitor mentees' engagement in targeted programs through encouragement and practice. Blended models harness the growing number of rigorously developed technology-delivered interventions, particularly those available through mobile apps. Although youth often struggle to stick with technology-delivered interventions on their own, their engagement deepens when it is blended with reminders, coaching, and face-to-face support that a mentor can provide. Blended mentoring models, which Big Brothers Big Sisters of America has already begun to embrace, have the potential to revolutionize how targeted, evidence-based interventions are delivered in large, nonspecific programs. In addition to reducing the risks inherent in a service model that hinges on the regular, ongoing service of volunteers, the embedded and blended approaches reduce costly investments in training programs, enabling large nonspecific mentoring programs to focus on what they do best: recruiting, screening, training, and supervising a helpful volunteer workforce.

In the final chapters, I ask readers to consider formal mentoring within a broader continuum of care and support. Given their limited supply, volunteer mentors should be allocated to those youth whose needs and circumstances require relatively structured support. For all other youth, including those transitioning out of formal mentoring programs, I discuss the value of encouraging youth to recruit teachers, coaches, and other caring adults in their everyday lives (i.e., natural mentors). As described in Chapter 9, natural mentors are far more common (roughly 70 percent of young people can identify at least one) than formal mentors (fewer than 5 percent of young people are ever assigned one), and are linked to an impressive range of positive outcomes.[13] Unfortunately, although marginalized youth stand to gain substantially more than their more privileged peers from the support and advocacy of well-connected, caring adults, they are far less likely to find them.[14] As class-based segregation increases and the top 10 percent of families peel away and consolidate their wealth and connections, this divide in "social capital" (i.e., the set of connections that provides support, motivation, and opportunities) is only widening. Fortunately, a new wave of *youth-initiated mentoring* models has emerged in recent years that teach young people how to recruit and sustain thriving networks of caring adults who can serve as important bridges to school and work.

Throughout this book, I hope to shed light on how adults can be most helpful to youth in a society marked by growing inequality. Each year, millions more children and adolescents, through no fault of their own, are born or thrust into poverty, where exposure to toxic levels of stress imperils their capacity to lead healthy and productive lives. If deployed wisely, both formal mentors and natural mentors represent a potentially important form of social capital that can help protect and promote the well-being of youth while galvanizing support for social and economic justice. But let's start at the beginning, when a generous young man happened to glance out his window and see a boy in need.

I

"The Kind of Justice Which Only a Brother Can Give"

On the morning of July 4, 1903, a random act of kindness by a twenty-two-year-old whiskey salesman launched the first American youth mentoring movement. "It was the Fourth of July," recalled Irv Westheimer decades later, "and I was down at my office between Third and Fourth on Walnut in Cincinnati." Young Irv was pacing his office, absentmindedly looking out a back window facing an alley, when he noticed a boy reach into a container of garbage, pull out a piece of bread, and then break off a piece to give to his dog, which, Irv recalled, "was an erstwhile white dog, and it seemed to me this wasn't exactly an ideal way for a young man to be eating."[1] Irv closed his rolltop desk, put on his hat, and walked out of his building toward the alley. "The boy was trembling with fear that I was going to beat him or do him some harm because that's all he knew." Irv talked quietly and gently to the boy: "Don't be frightened, I'm your friend. My name's Irv, what's your name?" "Tom," the boy responded. Hoping to put the boy at ease, Irv asked Tom the name of his dog. "That really had an effect on him, that I was interested enough to ask what his dog's name was, and he thought, well, after all, maybe I wasn't too bad. So I walked over to him gradually so as not to frighten him too much and I said, 'I'm going to have something to eat, and why don't you come along?' He didn't answer me, but I put my arm around his shoulders and we went over to Foucar's [Café]. In those days, you could get a glass of beer for a nickel, and you could get a big glass of beer for a dime, and a free corned beef sandwich."

Along with Tom's dog, Gyp, the pair walked along the Erie Canal, past churches, community halls, and streets of Cincinnati. To Tom, entering Foucar's must have been like stepping into an enchanted forest. Irv removed his hat and waved to the men seated at the grand marble and mahogany bar as he and Tom made their way to the dining room. The polished black oak walls were lined with mounted elk heads and shelves of beer steins, and a large stone fireplace framed the far end of the dining room. At a long, communal table, Tom and Irv shared the first of many lunches. As Irv recalls, Tom was no ordinary boy. He was smart and curious with a spark of joy that seemed to transcend his bleak circumstances. By the time their sandwiches arrived, Tom was talking cheerily to a delighted Westheimer about his dog and family. Charmed, Irv asked if he could walk Tom home to "see what his conditions were."

Irv knew that many families were living in crowded tenements mere blocks from his office, but nothing prepared him for what he saw. "I found out he was one of five children, with a single mother. His father was unknown—whether he was divorced, dead, gone or what, they didn't seem to know—the mother holding a miserable job, trying to keep her flock alive, didn't have time to look for another job even."

The image of Tom and his family, hungry and living in a crowded tenement, haunted Irv. He spent the next few days calling business associates and lining up a better-paying job for Tom's mother, as well as a job for Tom's oldest sister. Still, something about young Tom kept drawing him back, and Irv began stopping by before work to take him to the Cincinnati Jewish Center to help him meet new people and broaden his worldview. Within days, Tom had made friends with the sons and daughters of many of Cincinnati's successful businessmen. He won over the center staff and, as Irv recalled, "immediately the other workers at the Jewish Center saw a metamorphosis" in Tom. "He was gaining confidence and thinking about his future."

Hooked on the simple idea of providing opportunities and friendship to children in desperate need, Irv began proselytizing about the idea to the Jewish Center staff and other members of the business community. "It wasn't hard to find Little Brothers, in those days we didn't have any kind of unemployment insurance," he remembered. Within one week, twenty-five pairs had been made, "and that," concluded Irv, "was the birth of the Big Brothers movement." Of course, Irv was not content to let the matter rest there. On his many business trips to other cities, he asked his local contacts to assemble groups of young businessmen whom he could address. He would then extol the virtues of being a Big Brother and, he recalled, the men were "so delighted that we'd give them some concrete, specific direction where they could help. I had no trouble starting Big Brother movements, like Johnny Appleseed, wherever I went. Incidentally, it was the boys themselves who coined the phrase 'Big Brother and Little Brother.' They started saying, 'Here comes my big brother.' That's exactly what happened, and that's the way it got the name Big Brother movement." By 1910, the Big Brothers of Cincinnati was formally established.

At around the same time as Irv's first encounter with Tom, a similar story was unfolding in New York City. Ernest Kent Coulter, a young court clerk, had grown frustrated with the endless parade of "delinquent" boys sent through his court system. Boys who had done little more than steal a piece of fruit were herded into his courtroom and tried as adults. As Coulter saw it, the boys were victims— forced by their impoverished circumstances to drop out of school so they could be sent to work in factories where physical, sexual, and emotional abuse often occurred. Over time, Coulter became convinced that a society that "warps, thwarts, and denies the future citizen['s]" basic rights is to blame, and that "every crowded, ill-ventilated tenement is a tax upon the future." Coulter eventually became a strong advocate for juvenile court reform and believed that, if combined with the caring involvement of middle-class adults, such reforms would be infinitely more helpful for destitute boys than treating them as criminals.[2] Consequently, the early roots of Big Brothers Big Sisters were intertwined with the juvenile court reform movement.

Coulter disseminated a compelling idea to his Protestant Club business and community leaders at a New York gathering in 1904: "If each of you were to be neighbor, brother, to one of these little ones and see him through, forty would be saved from shipwreck. It is not law the lad needs, but justice, the kind of justice which only a brother can give—the love, the friendship, for which his life has been starving. All the rest will come on the trail of that."[3] He ended his speech with a plea: "To look after him, to help him do right, to make the little chap feel that there is at least one human being in this great city who takes a personal interest in him, who cares whether he lives or dies. I call for a volunteer."[4] By the end of the day, thirty-nine men had volunteered to serve as Big Brothers in New York City.

As the notion of befriending delinquent and destitute boys spread across the cities of the East Coast, Big Brothers was formalized into a national organization. New York's most elite philanthropic circles soon became involved. By June 1912, Big Brothers was active in twenty-six cities, serving mostly white children and families. Various women's groups across the country were also pairing women with girls. By 1916, Big Brothers and Big Sisters chapters could be found in ninety-eight cities across the United States, each following the same general model of matching impoverished children with middle-class adults and helping the children and their families navigate adversity.[5] Although Big Brothers and Big Sisters shared similar goals and approaches, it took until 1977 for the organizations to merge.

In the early 1900s, programs were seemingly springing up overnight because, according to Coulter, the model's "simplicity [and] its humanity, are the elements which make its appeal universal."[6] And, as Coulter made clear, society, not the child, was to blame for the situation the children were in: "We are learning day by day that the chief trouble has not been with the child, but with ourselves. The chief tenet in the faith of the Big Brothers and the Big Sisters, is that the condition of the tenement child is not of his own making." Coulter disagreed with the prevailing negative views about impoverished children and the punishing court system that treated children as adults. Rather, he viewed children in this situation with compassion, assigning blame for poor childhood outcomes to the family and the community. He described the way Big Brothers visited their boys' "ramshackle houses" as dangerous rescue missions, where when the Big Brothers "climb the black, creaky stairs" a drunken voice sometimes answered their knock with a gruff: "What yer want?" Echoing the initial actions of Irv Westheimer, Coulter also emphasized mentors' broader efforts to secure housing, jobs, and other resources for the youth and their families. He described a volunteer who stepped in when saw that his Little Brother's single mother was dying and his siblings were cold, sick, and hungry. Coulter wrote: "The tubercular mother and her small family were moved into three bright, clean rooms. Work was obtained for the older brother. The smaller boy was placed back in school. The mother is alive today and the 'little brother' of that day has developed into a splendid, manly fellow, with considerable artistic ability." In another instance, a Big Brother arrived at his mentee's apartment at night to find his Little Brother waiting outside in the cold with his siblings for their turn to sleep in the family's only bed. As Coulter explained, "The family was helped to get into larger, brighter, airier quarters, too, with good results." Other anecdotes tell of Big Brothers buying shoes, coats, and work clothes for the jobs that they helped their Little Brothers obtain and arranging medical care for their Little Brothers' siblings. Such actions helped to frame children's delinquency and other problems as symptoms of the grinding poverty of the day, along with exploitative child labor practices, crowded immigrant family tenements, and society's gaps in wealth and opportunity. Since struggles were thought to stem from limited opportunities, early Big Brothers Big Sisters volunteers behaved more like social workers who secured additional services for their Littles than the once-a-week, lighter touch, short-term mentors common today.

The conditions in the early 1900s were especially harsh for black families and immigrants. With the loss of Reconstruction-era protections, southern blacks were stripped of rights and economic opportunity, and racial segregation was on the rise. Meanwhile, in northern cities, low wages and poor labor conditions had consigned many immigrant families to poverty. By the time Theodore Roosevelt assumed his presidency in 1901, outrage over both the concentration of wealth and the corporate influence in politics had stirred a reform movement known as Progressivism. While Progressives were relatively less involved with black families, there was mounting concern over the conditions of the urban poor, especially children and immigrants in northern industrial cities. Support came from Protestant denominations that encouraged missionaries or "friendly visitors" to provide direct relief and prayer to lead to the "moral elevation of the poor," but the Progressive movement also included broader efforts like child labor laws, educational reforms, vocational guidance, and the development of a juvenile court system.[7] Many poor families were served through settlement houses, which had begun to spring up in the crowded centers of immigrant neighborhoods in industrialized cities in the late 1800s. Founded by Progressive activists and funded by charitable and religious groups, settlement houses were based on the idea that the difficulties facing poor families were interconnected and needed to be approached holistically. Many settlement houses were equipped with classrooms and meeting halls, as well as living spaces and communal dining facilities for the dozen or more middle-class "settlers" or residents, many of whom were artists, clergy, professors, and students.[8] By the early 1900s, there were more than one hundred settlement houses in the United States, a number that eventually quadrupled as the idea and funding expanded. As settlement houses gained influence, and the "settlers" learned more about the housing struggles and harsh working conditions facing poor families, settlers increasingly pushed for political reforms. This included advocating for a juvenile court system with probation officers, as well as state and federal legislation that could redress social and economic inequality and the massive concentration of wealth in a small number of families that characterized the early twentieth century.

Today, we may think of some of the wealthiest men to emerge from this Gilded Age (such as Rockefeller, Carnegie, and Vanderbilt) with appreciation for their charitable legacies, but many of these men were held in deep contempt at that time. Rockefeller, who founded Standard Oil in the late 1800s, was, according to historian Jill Lepore, "one of the most despised men in America, a symbol of everything that had gone wrong with industrialism."[9] A growing labor movement was forming and the public was demanding income taxes, a breakup of trusts and monopolies, and an end to the corrupting influence of money in American politics. Under the leadership of President Theodore Roosevelt, a national spirit of citizenship and charity took hold. Some of today's demands for economic reform seem mild when compared to Roosevelt's calls for Americans to advocate for equality of opportunities with a "fighting edge." As Theodore Roosevelt put it:

> That is what you fought for in the Civil War, and that is what we strive for now. At many stages in the advance of humanity, this conflict between the men who possess more than they have earned and the men who have earned more than they possess is the central condition of progress. . . . At every stage, and under all circumstances, the essence of the struggle is to equalize opportunity, destroy privilege, and give to the life and citizenship of every individual the highest possible value both to himself and to the commonwealth.[10]

It was in this period—when calls for both equality and volunteerism were in the zeitgeist—that everyday citizens became ad hoc champions of the less-advantaged children in their cities.

Over time, particularly after the onset of the Great Depression, the federal government began to enact more progressive economic policies aimed at strengthening the middle class. By the late 1930s, the wealth gap had substantially decreased. Broad public support for Progressive policies remained steady throughout much of the twentieth century, and many families enjoyed rising wages and wealth security. Although job opportunities were unequally distributed, the US economy saw the growth of a thriving middle class in the years after World War II, and rising productivity led to increased wages for most American workers in subsequent decades. By the 1960s and 1970s, the War on Poverty, the Great Society, and the civil rights and women's movements had begun to break down some of the social and economic barriers to equality.

Starting in the late 1970s, however, income inequality and wealth disparities began to grow again and have now reached levels not seen since the 1920s.[11] As the federal government cut tax rates for the wealthy and workers' bargaining power declined, income inequality soared and public support for welfare programs decreased. In his book *The Unwinding,* George Packer describes the "large currents" that led to societal changes in this period:

> Deindustrialization, the flattening of average wages, the financialization of the economy, income inequality, the growth of information technology, the flood of money into Washington, the rise of the political right—all had their origins in the late 70s. . . . The institutions that had been the foundation of middle-class democracy, from public schools and secure jobs to flourishing newspapers and functioning legislatures, were set on the course of a long decline.[12]

It was amid this decline that youth mentoring programs were embraced as a relatively cost-efficient, nongovernmental solution to delinquency and other related problems facing at-risk youth.

Whereas the first youth mentoring movement unfolded during the Progressive era and centered on the need to create better conditions for poor families, the youth mentoring movement that became increasingly popular in the late 1980s fixed its gaze more squarely on the child. In doing so, it defined the scope of the problem (a lack of role models) and solution (deployment of mostly middle-class volunteers) in ways that fit neatly with the more conservative "pull-yourself-up-by-the-bootstraps" ethos of the time.

To the extent that the mentoring movement of the late 1980s considered families and communities in the equation, it sometimes saw them as posing potential threats from which the child could be plucked, rather than homes and neighborhoods in which to invest resources.[13] This understanding also aligned with a growing scientific literature about the negative effects of cultural deprivation that had gained credibility in the latter half of the twentieth century.[14] More specifically, sensory studies that found that animals raised in stark circumstances fared worse than those in enriched environments were extended to address so-called cultural deficiencies in humans.[15] Everything from children's toys to the number of spoken words at home was seen as perpetuating cycles of poverty.[16] Whereas middle-class mothers were advised to minimize daycare hours to ensure secure attachments with their children, far less sentimentality was granted to poor mothers. Mentoring and other social programs were seen as compensatory efforts that could expose low-income, often black children to middle-class habits and values.[17] More generally, the notion that a straightforward, inexpensive, volunteer-based solution could address the needs of our nation's youth held enormous political appeal to those wary of governmental solutions.[18]

An important tipping point for this second wave of mentoring programs occurred in the mid-1990s when researchers at Public / Private Ventures in Philadelphia published an impact study of Big Brothers Big Sisters of America.[19] The study included over a thousand youth who applied to one of eight urban Big Brothers Big Sisters programs. The evaluators tracked the experiences over time of youth given access to the program *and* compared them to a control group that was placed on a waitlist. After eighteen months, the two groups were compared on various outcomes. Although the study indicated that the overall beneficial effects of the mentoring programs were slight, the researchers' report was embraced in policy and academic circles, and the widespread publicity that it received was an impetus for what flourished into a wider mentoring movement. Although negligible, the findings provided the scientific justification for policymakers and practitioners from across the political spectrum to promote mentoring. They were cited on the floor of the US Senate, and in research, news, and opinion pieces. Riding the public tide of enthusiasm, Big Brothers Big Sisters tripled in size within less than a decade of the study's release.[20]

To some, this Public / Private Ventures study served as a rebuke to the first randomized study of youth mentoring, the 1936 longitudinal Cambridge-Somerville Youth Study, which examined the effects of providing youth at risk for delinquency with relationships and services that were coordinated by paid counselors. In a thirty-year follow-up study of the participants, published in 1978, researcher Joan McCord found no benefits and, in some cases, even negative results for those who had had mentors, including arrests, health problems, and worse vocational outcomes.[21] McCord suggested a range of possible explanations for the counterintuitive findings (e.g., peer contagion, stigma, and feelings of loss). Youth mentoring was just one of several services provided to youth in the Cambridge-Somerville Youth Study, but the results raised questions about whether youth mentoring programs were as effective as had been assumed.[22]

Although the findings of the Public/Private Ventures study of Big Brothers Big Sisters programs in the mid-1990s appeared far more promising, researchers began to wonder how much of a difference the programs really made. One fact that was essentially lost in public discussion of the study was that youth in *both* groups (i.e., the mentored and the youth in the control groups) showed declining academic, behavioral, and psychosocial adjustment over time. The difference was a matter of degree—youth with mentors declined slightly less than the control group. Effect sizes varied considerably, depending on the characteristics of the individuals involved and the relationships formed, but they were generally small.[23] Moreover, a reanalysis of the data revealed that the youth who were in mentoring relationships that terminated within six months were doing worse than their counterparts in the control groups on a small number of variables, even after controlling for possible self-selection bias.[24]

To put these results in perspective, they were sufficiently unimpressive that, had the Big Brothers Big Sisters effects emerged during a Stage I clinical trial for a proposed new drug, the trial most likely would have been scrapped in lieu of alternative approaches. But that didn't happen. Mentoring was an idea whose time had come, and the evaluation won the hearts and minds of powerful constituents who were already primed for stories of healing through connection and for private-sector solutions.

In the mid-1990s, Congress authorized the Juvenile Mentoring Program (JUMP) within the Department of Justice to support mentoring for youth at risk for delinquent behavior and dropping out of school. Additional support grew from the 1997 Presidents' Summit for America's Future, which General Colin Powell chaired and which was attended by several prominent politicians, including President Clinton, former presidents Bush and Carter, governors, and mayors, as well as former first lady Nancy Reagan and notable business leaders. The summit facilitated pledges to create two million new mentoring relationships by the year 2000. Meanwhile, many smaller mentoring program organizations announced vigorous growth goals.

In the mid-1990s, Big Brothers Big Sisters was serving approximately one hundred thousand matches but set a goal of reaching nearly half a million youth by 2005, and a million by 2010. The Corporation for National and Community Service saw and raised the ante, calling for three million new youth mentoring matches by 2010.[25] Big Brothers Big Sisters' near century-long monopoly began to dissolve with the rise of a new crop of mentoring programs, many of which strayed in format, length, volunteer selection criteria, and goals from the original Big Brothers Big Sisters recipe.[26] Scores of new mentoring programs were launched from the mid-1980s through the early 2000s, attracting a growing pool of volunteers.[27] This enthusiasm also helped to expand the work of advocacy organizations, most notably the One to One Partnership (now MENTOR: The National Mentoring Partnership) founded earlier in the decade by businessmen Geoffrey Boisi and Ray Chambers.[28] MENTOR has since grown into a potent dissemination engine that provides training materials and technical assistance to its many affiliates in the United States. With the help of MENTOR's early advocacy, mentoring became, in the words of one policy expert, "the single most publicly talked about, written about, and broadly popular social intervention to improve the lives of disadvantaged youth."[29]

The early 2000s saw a further, precipitous jump in funding. This was made available through a widening array of federal, state, and private sources.[30] By 2004, the US Department of Health and Human Services and the Department of Education were allocating a collective $100 million per year for youth mentoring programs to support two large federal initiatives, the Mentoring Children of Prisoners program and the Student Mentoring Program. Although by the late 1990s youth mentoring was being characterized by its advocates as a "proven strategy," a series of meta-analyses of youth mentoring programs showed that the actual effects of youth mentoring remained disappointing, essentially unchanged even with the infusion of increased resources and research findings over time (see Figure 1.1).[31]

These stubbornly modest effects were largely obscured by more promising messages. Under the tacit assumption that mentoring programs were universally beneficial to youth, programs were increasingly pressured by funders to put their limited resources into launching new matches, sometimes at the expense of supporting existing ones. Recruiting new mentors remains one of the costliest investments that programs make, second only to training.[32] In a climate of heightened pressure to reduce the number of youth on waitlists, overburdened staff members sometimes fell prey to trivializing relationships out of necessity. Even more troubling, since volunteer recruitment was the rate-limiting factor in program growth, many programs were compelled to relax volunteer training requirements. They kept case management to a minimum by employing strategies such as conducting only email check-ins or making perfunctory bimonthly phone calls. Although these and other trends reduced the burdens on mentoring programs and volunteers, they were at odds with the types of practices (e.g., extensive upfront

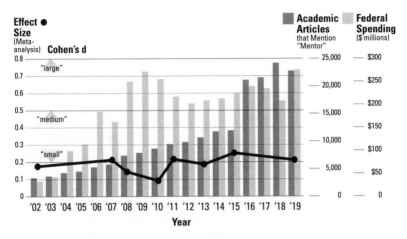

FIGURE I.I: TRENDS IN MENTORING EFFECTS 2002–2019: Meta-analyses of youth mentoring programs spanning nearly eighteen years show a consistent and relatively modest range of overall effects over time despite growth in mentor-related research and spending.

training, careful supervision, and outreach to caregivers) that help to establish and sustain high-quality mentoring relationships.[33]

This rapid expansion of formal youth mentoring programs also meant that programs had to cast ever wider nets to find volunteers.[34] To keep up with growth demands, programs even began to enlist high school students to serve as mentors to younger students. By the mid-2000s, nearly 45 percent of the school-based mentors in Big Brothers Big Sisters programs were high school students and an additional 20 percent were college students—groups that were not typically used in community programs and whose mentoring, research suggested, tended to result in smaller positive outcomes for the mentees.[35] In general, although nearly half of all mentoring relationships were not making it to the expected closure date, the disappointment of the mentees whose mentoring relationships didn't work out was overshadowed by the more compelling success stories.[36]

So, in a nutshell—a more conservative political zeitgeist and small but promising effects from the evaluation of a year-long, community-based approach to mentoring helped to galvanize a second-wave youth mentoring movement and stimulate aggressive growth goals. These goals, in turn, necessitated that mentoring be delivered more widely, which eventually transformed the intervention into something that bore a decreasing resemblance to earlier, intensive community-based models. Enthusiasm and advocacy eclipsed more sobering evaluation findings. As psychologists David Baker and Colleen Maguire concluded in 2005, "for most of the 20th century, despite high hopes, deep conviction, and strong belief, mentoring in America remained a largely unproven intervention."[37] As we will see in Chapter 2, researchers and evaluators have continued to struggle to produce findings to support these hopes, convictions, and beliefs. Youth mentoring continues to strike deep emotional chords and has attracted powerful constituents who, at some level, continue to look to evaluations and studies of youth mentoring to confirm what they intuitively hold to be true. Likewise, program practitioners understandably value straightforward findings that can directly guide their day-to-day efforts. It has been difficult to satisfy such appetites while remaining true to the evidence. But, if we want to create programs that truly help children, we need to take accurate stock of the effectiveness of existing programs and develop a more complete understanding of what it takes to deliver high-quality youth mentoring. That is my goal for this book.

2

MENTORING BY THE NUMBERS

How effective are youth mentoring programs? To answer this, researchers typically compare children and adolescents who have been paired with mentors to those who are on waitlists or in different programs. Depending on the mentoring program's goals, evaluators might look to see whether mentored youth show better school performance or better mental health, behavior, and / or social outcomes. To make such determinations, they might compare school records or ask both mentored and nonmentored youth and their parents or teachers to complete questionnaires before and after the programs.

To date, most evaluations of youth mentoring programs have been conducted in the United States, though a growing number of international mentoring program evaluations have been published in recent years. Mentoring programs in the United States have a different flavor from those in other countries. In contrast to the American mentoring movement, in which concerns about inequality and delinquency have been major drivers of program expansion, anxieties about the influx of migrants and refugees into linguistically and culturally homogeneous communities have motivated the expansion of programs across Europe and Asia, where mentoring is often seen as a tool to foster the social inclusion of immigrants and refugees.[1] Evaluations of these and other international mentoring efforts are included in several summaries presented below.

So, how effective is youth mentoring? To answer this, I review many large-scale evaluations, return-on-investment (ROI) studies (i.e., cost-benefit analyses), and meta-analyses that synthesize the results of numerous evaluations. Collectively, this review encompasses hundreds of evaluations and literally tens of thousands of youth. After summarizing findings from these three sources of evaluation, I compare mentoring interventions to other youth prevention interventions (such as recreational programs and social-emotional learning programs) as well as child and adolescent psychotherapy.

Since the quality and type of measurement strategies can vary widely across studies, program outcomes are typically presented in terms of a standardized "effect size" (i.e., the magnitude of impact) when making comparisons across studies. For simplicity, I present most findings in this book in terms of Cohen's d, which is a standardized index for effect size that represents the difference between youth in the treatment group (i.e., the mentored group) and youth who have been assigned to the control group or a different intervention. While there are no easy conventions, a standardized mean difference in the range of 0.20 or less is considered small, 0.50 is considered medium / moderate, and 0.80 or higher is considered large.[2] It will be helpful to keep these numbers in mind as I refer to effect sizes throughout the entire book. I will also contextualize these effect sizes using guidelines that have been derived across comparable outcome measures from comparable intervention areas, populations, and risk levels.[3]

Program Evaluations

Since the landmark evaluation of Big Brothers Big Sisters' community-based mentoring programs in the mid-1990s discussed in Chapter 1, three additional large-scale randomized controlled trial evaluations of nonspecific, "friendship" mentoring program models (i.e., programs primarily focused on building strong relationships / not generally targeted to particular youth or outcomes) have been conducted.[4] Because these studies have shown some promising (albeit small) differences between the mentored and the control groups on a range of youth outcomes, they have helped to maintain enthusiasm for the expansion of the field of youth mentoring.[5] Other community-based mentoring programs, such as Friends of the Children, have continued this pattern, drawing on relatively modest positive effects to justify ambitious expansion efforts.[6]

Several evaluations of school-based mentoring have revealed similarly modest effects. Since 2007, three large experimental evaluations of mentoring programs in schools have been conducted, including a study of Big Brothers Big Sisters programs. All of these evaluations have revealed relatively small positive outcomes in the short term, which have tended to decrease in the longer term.[7] Moreover, although the programs share similar goals, they have not produced a consistent (and therefore predictable) set of outcomes. For example, the primary outcomes reported in evaluations of nonspecific, community-based mentoring programs have been largely nonoverlapping, ranging from effects on drugs and alcohol use, aggression, and truancy to effects on depression, conduct problems, perceived support, and depression; and indicators of well-being, such as hope and optimism.[8]

There have also been several evaluations of programs more targeted in their theoretical models and mentoring practices than the
more common *nonspecific* programs that focus on building friendships through activities and conversations. A review of the existing
literature offers preliminary evidence for the promise of these more
targeted approaches to youth mentoring (see Figure 2.1).[9] In fact, decades of large-scale evaluation data suggest that targeted mentoring programs are producing effects that are well above the overall
average effects for mentoring programs (0.21) reported in meta-
analyses (and discussed below), while many of the most trusted
nonspecific programs are producing effects well below the average
overall effect. These targeted programs often incorporate goal-
setting skills and between-session homework, while also allowing
time for recreational, relationship-building activities. For example,
the three largest mean effect sizes, as shown in Figure 2.1, involved
mentors trained to teach perspective-taking and social skills
(Karcher, Davis, and Powell); teach cognitive-behavioral techniques
(Jent and Niec); and engage students with disabilities in *skills
training* activities around science, technology, engineering, and
math (STEM) (Sowers et al.), all within the context of developing a
friendship between mentor and mentee.[10] Other programs with
strong effects have adopted similarly balanced models in which the
primary focus is on skill-building activities integrated with
relationship-building activities.[11] The relationship-building helps to
cultivate rapport, increases youth engagement, and serves as a cat-
alyst to strengthen the intervention.[12]

The main limitation of these evaluations, however, is their relatively small samples of youth. Moreover, the evaluations of the targeted programs benefit from the fact that they measure a restricted
range of outcomes more directly aligned with the treatment goals.

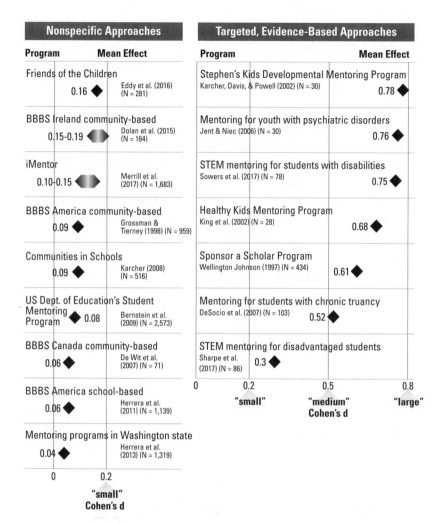

FIGURE 2.1: NONSPECIFIC VERSUS MORE TARGETED, EVIDENCE-BASED MENTORING APPROACHES: Historically, small positive effects have justified the continued use of nonspecific mentoring approaches. However, several evaluations have demonstrated that targeted, evidence-based mentoring approaches can achieve more substantial effects.

In nonspecific programs, widely diverse outcomes are calculated into overall averages in ways that can obscure or wash out selective improvements.[13] And, since no randomized trials comparing the effects of nonspecific to targeted program models have been conducted to date, we are left with many other variables (e.g., sample, program size and length, and implementation quality) that could account for different effect sizes across these types of programs. Finally, there are also plenty of examples of targeted mentoring models that have produced relatively small effects.[14] Thus, although the bulk of the published data may support more targeted programs, there are certainly instances in which this is not the case. At the same time, years of evaluations indicate the majority of nonspecific models produce overall effects below 0.10, and I know of no instances in which nonspecific program models have achieved effects in the range of the more promising targeted, evidence-based models.

Meta-analysis

Meta-analysis combines the results of multiple individual evaluations (such as those reviewed above) in ways that can produce more reliable and precise impact estimates and permit comparisons across approaches and characteristics. For example, researchers have been able to test whether boys are more responsive to mentoring than girls (the findings are mixed, though recent studies do seem to suggest that boys may derive additional benefits) and whether mentoring affects some outcomes (e.g., academic performance) more than others (e.g., delinquency).[15] These meta-analyses have produced mixed findings, with the most recent comprehensive meta-analysis showing no differential effects.[16] It should be noted, however, that effects are often derived from very different types of programs and the ability to make comparisons depends on the information provided in the original evaluations. Additionally, meta-analyses examine overall program characteristics (e.g., the percentage of college-aged mentors in programs) and cannot specify the particular strategies employed by individuals or subgroups.

Some of these meta-analyses have focused on specific subsets of youth, settings, or populations. For example, meta-analyses of youth at risk for delinquent or aggressive behavior have revealed a small, but significant, impact of mentoring on reducing juvenile reoffending and delinquency.[17] One meta-analysis found that youth mentoring programs showed smaller effects on most outcomes than did mentoring programs for young adults in the workplace or in higher education settings.[18] Other studies have taken a broader look at the field. For example, two comprehensive meta-analyses of youth mentoring showed small, but significant, effects of mentoring across outcomes.[19] Most recently, a meta-analysis from 2019 of seventy intergenerational, one-on-one mentoring program evaluations that were conducted from 1975 through 2017 and represented more than twenty-five thousand youth once again showed that mentoring yielded a range of significant, but overall small, effects.[20] The findings were, in fact, remarkably consistent with past comprehensive meta-analyses of youth mentoring, despite the inclusion of more recent evaluations and despite steady investments in research to improve program design. Taken together, these meta-analyses provide modest support for the effectiveness of one-on-one, caring relationships with adults, but they continue a trend line of relatively small effect sizes that has not markedly improved in nearly twenty years.

After completing the first of the major meta-analyses of youth mentoring discussed above, DuBois et al. observed that the reality of mentoring programs was "not necessarily consistent with the manner in which results of the large-scale evaluation frequently have been cited by the media as demonstrating a large impact for mentoring relationships."[21] Seventeen years later, the findings from the 2019 meta-analysis, also referenced above, led its authors to call for "more rigorous adherence to evidence-based practices that target specific mechanisms underlying particular youth difficulties, rather than relying on a relatively low-intensity, nonspecific approach with uneven adherence to practices that are research-informed."[22] Interestingly, the 2019 meta-analysis included studies that varied in rigor and intensity and whose findings ranged from negative effects to large positive effects.[23] Among the programs included in that meta-analysis, those with the smallest effects tended to be the large, nonspecific approaches while medium to large positive effects tended to be found in more targeted and skills-based programs (see Figure 2.2). Additionally, a recent meta-analysis revealed that targeted mentoring programs produced average effect sizes that were more than double those of nonspecific programs and were significantly more effective in improving school, psychological, and social functioning.[24] Thus, overall effect sizes in meta-analyses are likely being skewed by the relatively smaller number of targeted programs (serving far fewer youth) that are included in the analyses.

Return on Investment

Return on investment (ROI) studies or cost-benefit analyses provide another point of comparison for mentoring programs. To calculate an ROI, researchers estimate in dollars the benefits, or returns, yielded on a monetary investment. These benefits are typically

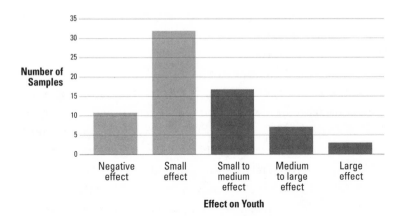

FIGURE 2.2: EFFECT SIZE RANGES IN A RECENT META-ANALYSIS: A 2019 meta-analysis of seventy evaluations of youth mentoring programs found that their effectiveness varied considerably. Those programs with medium to large positive effects tended to encompass more targeted, evidence-based approaches.

calculated by dividing the cost of a program to taxpayers by the value of the expected outcomes (e.g., lower drug use, higher graduation rates, and higher levels of employment) on lifetime wages. The Washington State Institute for Public Policy has provided one of the most comprehensive sets of ROI calculations for the youth mentoring field to date.[25] Collectively, these calculations indicate wide variations in the monetary returns of youth mentoring programs—in part because the approach and the effectiveness of the approach can vary so widely. There are several important caveats to keep in mind when interpreting these ROI comparisons. First, the Big Brothers Big Sisters evaluations have used larger samples and more rigorous methods (e.g., randomized control trials) than the smaller, more targeted interventions, and research in educational programs has found that greater methodological rigor is generally associated with smaller program effects.[26] Although different sub-sets of youth in large-scale, nonspecific programs may show strong benefits on certain outcomes, these peaks are flattened when calculating overall sample averages. Second, the Washington State Institute for Public Policy used average total cost estimates, which some consider to be less accurate than determining the marginal cost of adding new matches to a pre-existing program.[27] Third, improvements in nonquantifiable outcomes (such as emotional well-being, improved relationships, and life satisfaction) can have collateral economic benefits rarely included in ROI calculations.[28] More generally, extrapolated income and behavioral estimates are relatively crude measures of program effectiveness, and there is considerable uncertainty involved in estimating future earnings based on educational attainment.[29]

Although these ROI analyses do not explicitly compare nonspe-cific mentoring programs to targeted, evidence-based programs, their overall findings support the latter. For example, one such pro-gram with relatively high yields, Across Ages, specifically targeted youth at risk for drug involvement and matched them with adult volunteers who were equipped with a skills-based curriculum.[30] Another program with an impressive ROI, Sponsor-a-Scholar, tar-geted "middle-achieving" students (i.e., those with grades in the B–C range) at risk of not attending college, matched them with trained mentors, and provided consistent academic support for the ex-plicit goal of college admission and attendance.[31] Similarly, other mentoring programs that were evaluated included those that tar-geted youth with disruptive behavioral disorders, in which men-tors taught, coached, and reinforced problem-solving and other skills. Overall, evaluations of these latter programs, most of which appeared to target specific problems and populations, yielded positive returns—suggesting that their economic benefits outweigh their costs.

The analyses also revealed that school-based mentoring programs yielded negative ROIs. These analyses did not necessarily distinguish between programs that were nonspecific or targeted, so it is difficult to draw firm conclusions. That said, they were based on data that were collected during a period of time when the nonspecific models were more dominant.[32] In contrast, nonvolunteer school-based mentoring interventions (i.e., those delivered by teachers and staff rather than outside volunteers) yielded large, positive returns.[33] These programs targeted youth with demonstrated risk (e.g., disciplinary problems, truancy, or emerging mental health problems) and sought specific outcomes (e.g., reducing disciplinary problems and truancy and strengthening emotional self-regulation). These results are understandable given the specific targets and the fact that teachers and staff likely have relatively more training and experience with youth, and relatively more support in schools than do external volunteers. Although additional studies are needed, these analyses suggest that it may be more cost effective to draw on mentors who have already had some training, knowledge, and experience working with youth.

Taken together, evaluations, meta-analyses, and ROI studies have consistently shown that nonspecific, friendship models of mentoring are less effective than other approaches. And, although the evidence is more limited and additional experimental evaluations are needed, data suggest that more targeted interventions have the potential to yield markedly stronger effects and better investment returns.

Comparisons with Other Youth Interventions

When contrasting mentoring models, it is also instructive to examine the broader literature on relationship-based youth interventions, where the merits of more intuitive, nonspecific approaches versus more targeted, evidence-based approaches have also been debated and studied for years. Here, again, we find stronger support for more active, targeted forms of skills training. For example, a meta-analysis of twenty-eight studies of school-based interventions with elementary through high school students that were designed to promote social-emotional competence found that interventions using active approaches (e.g., role playing and skills building) yielded effect sizes that were *three times higher* than those using passive (e.g., conversational or instructional) approaches.[34]

The most compelling argument for the efficacy of more targeted, evidence-based approaches in interventions with youth can be found in the rich body of research on therapeutic helping relationships. There, debates have been simmering for decades as to whether helping relationships work due to nonspecific factors (such as the caliber of the therapist-patient relationship, therapist qualities, and client expectations and characteristics) or through approaches that combine the nonspecific factors with targeted evidence-based strategies and techniques.[35] Although support for the latter position continues to build, this debate is hardly settled.[36] As recently as a decade ago, proponents of evidence-based mental health treatment models bemoaned the fact that "despite compelling research support for the merits of specific interventions for specific problems, clinical psychology, as a field, has failed to embrace these treatments, to standardize their use through formal practice guidelines, to promote and disseminate them widely through training, or to ensure that they are available to the patients who need them."[37]

One silver lining to child and adolescent psychotherapists' continued embrace of nonspecific "usual care," that is, care in which they "use their clinical judgement as they [see] fit, not constrained by evidence-based interventions or manuals," is that it has permitted a wealth of comparisons with more targeted, evidence-based therapeutic approaches.[38] Such comparisons are relevant to debates in mentoring, as the more intuitive, improvisational usual-care approaches in psychotherapy are analogous to the nonspecific, friendship model in youth mentoring. (Although therapists may incorporate proven approaches in "usual care," they typically blend, modify, remix, and string them together based on their intuition.)

So how do these usual-care models compare to more targeted, evidence-based approaches? In recent years, several convincing reviews and meta-analyses have shown that child and adolescent therapy that more carefully follows evidence-based manuals and approaches produces relatively larger effects.[39] In 2005, psychologist John Weisz and his team conducted a meta-analysis of thirty-two randomized trials in youth psychotherapy, directly comparing "usual care" versus targeted, evidence-based approaches, and found that the latter outperformed the former. The mean effect sizes indicated that, on average, youth receiving evidence-based care were better off than 64 percent of youth receiving usual care.[40] Importantly, evidence-based care's "superiority was not reduced by high levels of youth severity or by inclusion of minority youths."[41] In what is perhaps an understatement, given the evidence produced across several studies, the authors of the meta-analysis concluded that, "in principle, it seems reasonable to favor interventions that have been tested empirically and shown to work."[42] Two subsequent meta-analyses led by the same researcher, psychologist John Weisz, also showed better outcomes for youth who received therapy using evidence-based rather than usual-care approaches.[43] After completing their most recent comparison of usual-care and evidence-based approaches, Weisz and his colleagues concluded that structured, evidence-based treatments, while showing room for improvement, are superior to intuitive, usual-care approaches in treating children and adolescents.[44]

The field of youth psychotherapy is sufficiently analogous to youth mentoring that it can offer valuable lessons about the relative benefits of nonspecific versus targeted, evidence-based approaches. Although direct experimental comparisons have yet to be conducted, decades of research suggest overall small effects for nonspecific, friendship approaches to youth mentoring relative to more targeted, evidence-based approaches. Nonetheless, the nonspecific model remains the most common approach in youth mentoring programs. In a large national survey of 1,271 mentoring programs serving nearly half a million mentees, program directors identified the most common goals as broad "life skills" (54 percent), "general youth development" (51 percent), and "providing a caring adult relationship" (44 percent), with comparatively fewer programs endorsing more specific and instrumental goals, such as college access (18 percent), violence prevention (5 percent), STEM education (6 percent), or substance use prevention (3 percent).[45] In an evaluation of Big Brothers Big Sisters school-based mentoring, only 11 percent of mentors endorsed having a specific instrumental goal (e.g., "academic improvement" or "improving school behavior"), while 79 percent endorsed broad developmental goals (e.g., "being a friend" or "helping the child feel good about him/herself").[46]

Understanding and Countering the Resistance

Evidence from evaluation, meta-analyses, and ROI studies all point to the value of targeted, evidence-based approaches to youth mentoring. Findings from decades of analogous research on youth psychotherapy have reached similar conclusions. Nonetheless, many in the youth mentoring field remain resistant to a more targeted, evidence-based approach. Because many continue to assume that formal mentoring programs have their impact primarily through nonspecific relationship processes, overly specific guidelines and highly structured goals can be seen as unnecessary. For example, in a 2012 article in the *American Journal of Orthopsychiatry,* Junlei Li and Megan M. Julian compared the mentor-mentee bond to that of fluoride in toothpaste: other ingredients (e.g., for color or taste) may add value, but they are not essential to the success of the match. The authors argued that the "enduring emotional attachment" is the only "active ingredient" in mentoring programs and that "scaled-up programs and policies serving children and youth often fall short of their potential impact when their designs or implementation drift toward manipulating other 'inactive' ingredients (e.g., incentive, accountability, curricula) instead of directly promoting developmental relationships."[47] Other researchers have reached similar conclusions, noting that "the common feature of successful interventions across all stages of the life cycle through adulthood is that they promote attachment and provide a secure base for exploration and learning for the child. Successful interventions emulate the mentoring environments offered by successful families."[48] This line of thinking also fits with my own earlier conceptual models, which suggested that such mentoring bonds can create "corrective experiences" that help young people through earlier relationship difficulties.[49]

Programs that view relationship-building as the central component to their success may actually devalue structure and goal-
setting, discouraging mentors from focusing on problems and
providing little upfront training to capitalize on their intuition
and natural capacities to build the strongest ties. Of course, in rare
cases, such long-term, less-targeted relationships can be truly transformative, providing mentees with a secure base from which to explore the world and manage challenges. But since mentoring programs cannot reliably reproduce and bottle this magic, a more
effective strategy would be to focus on improving the vast majority of relationships.

Proponents of nonspecific, friendship models of youth mentoring
have raised a host of other concerns, including questioning the extent to which targeted, evidence-based approaches can take race and
ethnicity into account. Yet studies of targeted therapy have generally shown no differential effects across racial and cultural backgrounds.[50] Still others argue that the virtue of many mentoring
programs is that they target a broad range of outcomes. Thus, the
lack of specificity is a feature, not a bug. Yet decades of child and
adolescent psychotherapy research has found that the "treatment
of multiple problems concurrently produces strikingly smaller mean
effects than treatment of any single target problem."[51] Of course,
problems can co-occur, so it is natural for programs to target several related risk and protective factors at once. The key distinction
here isn't simply the number of risk and protective factors that are
targeted, but whether they are targeted at all.

Other holdouts for nonspecific approaches argue that mentoring
programs provide an easy on-ramp to other care and services down
the road. However, given the high level of attrition in mentoring
relationships, particularly for the highest-risk youth, there is no

guarantee that mentoring can serve as an effective on-ramp. There are thus opportunity costs to not providing youth with the most effective services when the chance arises. Finally, some may argue that it is inherently difficult to quantify the effects of nonspecific approaches in the short term. Many evaluations depend on child self-reports of "soft" outcomes such as self-esteem, while other results may be undetected in the short term only to emerge later in life.[52] For example, although a thirty-year follow-up of the randomized Cambridge-Somerville Youth Study found negative long-term effects for mentoring, recent twenty-year follow-ups with the original 1995 Big Brothers Big Sisters sample indicate possible positive changes in a few social (but not economic) outcomes.[53]

These latent or "sleeper" effects may point to promising long-term effects from nonspecific approaches, and additional research is certainly warranted. If that is the case, however, it is likely that psychologically precise interventions would yield even greater long-term benefits, since such interventions can pinpoint and disrupt problems before they develop into more complicated issues. Given the choice, most parents and investors would likely give more support to programs that produce more immediate and predictable benefits than to those with a small number of effects that materialize many years or even decades later.

Previous critiques of youth mentoring have highlighted the relative imperviousness of the field to data, and the ways in which research findings are sometimes presented in misleading, overly optimistic terms.[54] Disappointing verdicts on our most common approaches to mentoring should no longer be interpreted as errant needles in the haystack, but as the last straws that catalyze our search for more effective models. The synthesis of data in this chapter lays bare decades of disappointing findings. We cannot continue to turn a blind eye, and we can do better. In making the case for employing targeted, evidence-based approaches, I am not suggesting that the mentor-youth relationship is unnecessary. Rather, I am arguing that a relationship alone is insufficient basis for a youth intervention model. In fact, as the field of mentoring corrects for an overemphasis on intuitive approaches and moves in more targeted, evidence-based directions, it should resist veering too far from what sets the field apart from pure tutoring or other skills-training classes: the catalyzing role of a caring relationship.[55] The key will be to find that equilibrium and to make corrections as needed.

3

How Did We Get It So Wrong for So Long?

Lee Sechrest, an expert on research methods, has argued that weak or nonexistent program outcomes (like those revealed in many mentoring evaluations) can be attributable to one or more of three explanations: "(1) some treatments are inherently weak and will do little for any condition (e.g., a single aspirin tablet); (2) some treatments are potentially strong, but are inappropriate for the specific condition (e.g., antibiotics used in the treatment of viral diseases); and (3) some treatments are potentially strong but are given in only a weak form (e.g., a small dose of penicillin to treat an infection)."[1]

All three of these explanations are at play in the field of youth mentoring. First, simply introducing intergenerational friendships, engaging in conversations and enjoyable recreational activities, and / or stringing together various approaches in unsystematic ways appears to represent a weak program model that will generally have very little bearing on measurable, short-term outcomes for youth in the absence of more active, rigorous intervention strategies. Second, some approaches may work for some youth but not effectively target the particular needs and circumstances of all of the youth that a program is serving. That is, although a subset of youth may benefit from the mere presence of caring and supportive adults, many youth need more than this. Moreover, even the most promising targeted, evidence-based approach will be of little use if it is not well-suited to the needs and circumstances of particular youth. This becomes apparent when mentoring programs take top-down, needs-blind approaches to implementing short-term initiatives—sometimes in response to funding opportunities—that are irrelevant for some fraction of youth in the program (i.e., insufficiently targeted models), ultimately driving down average program effects. Third, programs that adopt evidence-based practices well-matched to their target population may do so unevenly, with insufficient attention to the original, effective program model.[2] In mentoring, as in other interventions, straying too far from the original program guidelines when disseminating successful program models generally weakens the intervention's effects.[3]

A recent evaluation of program enhancements in community-based mentoring programs illustrates these interrelated explanations.[4] More than 800 youth were randomly assigned to either receive standard mentoring services or an enhanced mentoring intervention. In the enhanced version, mentors and program staff were trained in the theory and delivery of an intervention derived from research on "sparks" (i.e., discovering youth's hidden strengths and interests) and based on a growth mindset (i.e., construing abilities as malleable instead of fixed). At follow-up, the researchers found no differences between the standard and enhanced conditions across all measured youth outcomes, including outcomes in both subjective areas (e.g., growth mindset and intentional self-regulation) and behavioral areas (e.g., conduct problems and delin-

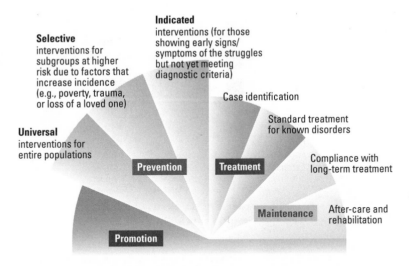

FIGURE 3.1: CONTINUUM OF INTERVENTIONS AND RISK IN MENTAL, EMOTIONAL, AND BEHAVIORAL DISORDERS AMONG YOUTH: Reformatted with permission of the National Academies Press from Patricia J. Mrazek and Robert J. Haggerty, eds., "Reducing Risk for Mental Disorders" (Washington, DC: National Academies Press, 1994), figure 2.1; permission conveyed through Copyright Clearance Center, Inc.

youth who enter mentoring programs are already experiencing marginalization and relatively high levels of risk and difficulty. For example, an analysis of the two million young people aged six through eighteen that Big Brothers Big Sisters of America has served over the past decade revealed that the majority were from low-income families (78 percent) and / or lived in single-parent homes (61 percent).[8] Similarly, a 2018 evaluation of 2,165 American youth participating in thirty nationally representative mentoring programs found that nearly 70 percent of mentees were from marginalized, nonmajority racial backgrounds.[9] The vast majority (85 percent) of the mentees' parents reported that their children had recently been exposed to

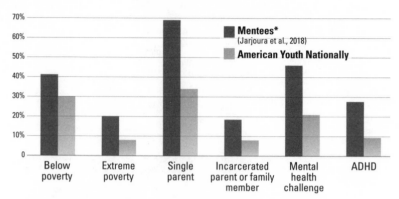

*Mentees in Jarjoura et al. (2018) ranged in age from 9 to 16, average age 12.4 at baseline.
National Data Resource: Kids Count Data Center, 2017 (except ADHD: Centers for Disease Control, 2016)

FIGURE 3.2: A POPULATION AT RISK: Youth who enter mentoring programs are more likely than average to be experiencing difficult life circumstances and behavioral and mental health issues.

family stress (such as a family member struggling with substance use, frequent family arguments, or homelessness), while more than three-quarters (76 percent) noted that their children faced economic adversity and safety concerns (such as housing insecurity, parental job instability, or gangs or drugs in the neighborhood), with participating families' median annual income ranging from $20,000 to $30,000. Compared to young people on average nationally, mentees were roughly twice as likely to live in extreme poverty, reside in a single-parent household, and have an incarcerated parent or family member (see Figure 3.2).[10]

Not surprisingly, given these life circumstances, many mentees were already struggling with relatively serious academic, social, and emotional difficulties.[11] At intake, more than half of parents (52 percent) reported that their child was struggling academically (e.g., failing or at risk for failing two or more classes / subjects in school, or missing school three or more times a month) and more than half (52 percent) also said that their child was having significant issues with peers (e.g., being bullied or not having any close friends). Nearly half the parents (46 percent) also reported that their child had mental health concerns (e.g., frequent sadness or being under the care of a mental health care provider). Lastly, roughly one in five parents (19 percent) reported that their child had exhibited problematic behavior (e.g., suspensions, substance use, or contact with police), a rate dramatically higher than national averages and one that is particularly alarming given that the average mentee was approximately twelve years old.[12] Finally, the referred youth were more than twice as likely as the average youth to be suffering from a mental health problem such as depression or anxiety, and three times more likely to have ADHD.[13] ADHD and related behavioral problems appear to take a particular toll on adult-youth relationships, but only about a quarter (27 percent) of the youth were receiving counseling or therapy, and even fewer were getting help at school (22 percent) or receiving medication for mental health struggles (20 percent).[14] Other studies have yielded similar trends. One research team found that a quarter of the youth in its large-scale evaluations reported high levels of depressive symptoms at baseline.[15]

Mentoring programs have simply been insufficiently targeted and intensive to address the acute risks described above. This has resulted in relatively small overall effects for mentoring programs, particularly relative to many other youth-serving prevention strategies.[16] In general, programs that work with youth who experience more acute behavioral, emotional, and academic problems tend to show stronger positive effects because, like a pendulum, there is more room for an upswing.[17] Despite this, mentoring programs yield relatively weaker effects than other interventions that serve youth at comparable levels of risk. Even single-session psychotherapy interventions for youth with psychiatric problems have yielded moderate effect sizes (0.32) notably larger than those found in long-term mentoring interventions.[18]

Likewise, compared to universal prevention programs serving lower-risk youth, youth mentoring programs produce below-average effects across most common outcomes. In an attempt to develop better benchmarks of universal youth intervention effects on specific outcomes, researchers recently pulled together seventy-four meta-analyses of universal prevention programs involving youth aged five through eighteen.[19] Mentoring program effects, while certainly within the range of the broader field of universal prevention, were on the lower end of the distribution for several outcomes including social relationships, externalizing and internalizing symptoms, and academic achievement.[20]

Despite the relatively high-risk profile of their mentees, many mentoring programs continue nonetheless to operate as universal prevention programs, offering recreation and enrichment to youth in need of more targeted care. Meanwhile, many parents and guardians, particularly those from marginalized backgrounds, are turning to mentoring programs in lieu of professional services to treat what are, in some cases, clinically significant psychosocial difficulties. In a survey of nearly 750 caregivers to adolescents, black caregivers were less likely than white caregivers to perceive the need for psychological counseling services for their adolescent, irrespective of symptom severity, and were more comfortable with informal service formats like mentoring.[21] In fact, the odds that black caregivers would report that their adolescent needed a mentoring program more than doubled when their child was struggling with behavioral or mental health problems. Likewise, in a recent study of Big Brothers Big Sisters Canada, 25 percent of parents identified their child's disability or psychiatric illness as a primary reason for referral to school-based mentoring programs.[22] This relative comfort with mentoring programs may stem from the significant barriers (including transportation, insurance, language differences, lack of knowledge/access, and stigmatization) that caregivers face in obtaining mental health and other services for their children. This is compounded for families of color, who are also more likely to experience mental health services and providers as discriminatory, coercive, culturally insensitive, and insufficiently attentive to structural and systemic inequality.[23] Although culturally competent services are growing, many marginalized communities and families remain understandably wary about treatment options.[24] Their children are still far more likely than those of affluent parents to receive medication as opposed to specialty behavioral or psychosocial intervention in response to emotional or behavioral struggles and, compared to white youth, youth of color have disproportionate rates of unmet mental health service needs.[25]

As described above, many mentoring programs are serving youth with significant emotional and behavioral struggles, and many parents and caregivers are turning to mentoring programs as a more accessible alternative to youth mental health services.[26] Yet, instead of targeting clear, measurable goals and providing careful training and adequate supervision to their volunteers, youth mentoring programs are often identifying vague goals and offering relatively little training, direction, and supervision.[27] In the majority of US mentoring programs, volunteers receive fewer than two hours of prematch training and often perfunctory supervision thereafter.[28] In typical mentoring programs, matches are overseen by caseworkers with large caseloads, making it difficult for them to intensively supervise individual matches.

What's more, even as many of the youth they serve are coping with acute issues, mentoring programs struggle to develop and implement meaningful match activities, leaving volunteers in the lurch about what exactly they and their mentees should do together.[29] My colleague Michael Karcher once observed that, like the friendly vultures in the classic Disney movie *The Jungle Book,* mentors often find themselves responding to their mentees' requests for activity ideas with something like, "I dunno, what do *you* wanna do?"[30]

Advocates of nonspecific, friendship approaches to youth mentoring might argue that whatever they eventually "wanna do," be it crafts, sports, or going to a museum, is likely to be a valuable experience because mentees' lives are so bereft of activities and adult involvement. Yet there is evidence that many mentees are already involved in extracurricular activities and other positive youth development programs when they sign up for mentoring programs. In the national survey of representative mentoring programs, the majority of mentees (87 percent) were already engaged in sports, clubs, and/or artistic activities when they entered the mentoring program.[31] Many were also enrolled in after-school activities (68 percent) and team sports (52 percent), while sizable proportions were involved in school clubs (40 percent), career services (43 percent), and community service (34 percent). Nearly a third of the matches met during after-school hours, which means that youth were likely being pulled from these organized activities to meet with their mentors. Thus, time spent with mentors often supplants youth engagement in other relationships or activities.

Others may argue that, irrespective of a program's approach, a caring adult is important because so many youth lack special adults in their lives. According to a recent national study of mentoring programs, however, the great majority of mentees (71 percent) enter the programs with at least one "special non-parent adult" already in their lives, a rate that is consistent with national youth surveys.[32] This suggests that children are being referred for reasons that go beyond recreation and adult support. Finding a mentoring program and enrolling one's child in it is not trivial. The process often involves completing applications, being interviewed, and enduring long waitlists. Particularly considering the high rates of mentees' baseline difficulties, as well as their involvement in positive youth development activities and relationships with natural mentors, it is likely that parents are looking for something more specific than a caring, fun-spirited adult when they seek out programs.

Underestimated youth risk combined with this mismatch between what mentees need, what volunteers are being asked to deliver, and what parents are looking for may also help to explain the high volunteer attrition rates that many youth mentoring programs experience, which can further drive down program impacts. Back in 1990, author Marc Freedman observed that "it's easier to get volunteers to sign up than to show up."[33] Twenty years later, in the age of digital distraction and a general devaluing of in-person conversations and connections, this issue appears to have only worsened. Columnist David Brooks has referred to the period we are living through as the "golden age of bailing," characterized by a lowering threshold for flaking out and cancelling plans.[34] We certainly see this trend in the high rates at which volunteers miss meetings and drop out early in many of today's mentoring programs.[35] In a study of over seven

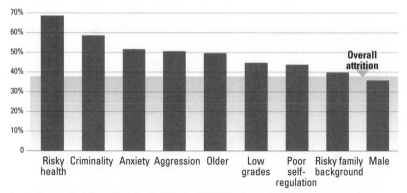

Source: Kupersmidt, J., Stump, K., Stelter, R., & Rhodes, J. (2017). Predictors of premature match closure in youth mentoring relationships. *American Journal of Community Psychology*, 59, 25–35.

FIGURE 3.3: MENTORING RELATIONSHIPS WITH HIGHER-RISK YOUTH ARE LESS ENDURING: When volunteers are matched with youth who are more at risk, the matches have a higher attrition rate than average.

thousand nationally representative Big Brothers Big Sisters matches, researchers found that overall attrition rates (i.e., relationships terminating before the agreed-upon end date) were close to 40 percent, with higher rates when volunteers were matched with youth facing more struggles (see Figure 3.3).[36] Although mentees sometimes end the relationships, the sad fact is that many well-intentioned mentors give up on youth who may stand to gain the most—those with relatively poor health, academic, social, or behavioral functioning—and such youth often have the shortest, least satisfying matches.[37]

These high rates of mentor attrition represent lost opportunities to intervene and are particularly troubling given that a relatively low percentage of adults are stepping up to volunteer in the first place. According to US census data, rates of volunteer commitment to calendar- or academic-year mentoring programs have remained relatively steady over the past decade, limited to only 2.5 million adults, or around 1 percent of the adult US population. Moreover, mentor retention from one year to the next has been steadily declining over the past decade.[38]

A high mentor attrition rate translates into a weaker dose of the intervention, which can diminish program outcomes. Given this, along with the potential for mentee disappointment and the costs involved in recruiting and training new mentors, it will be important to more fully acknowledge youth risk and to understand and staunch mentor attrition. In a recent survey of over one thousand mentoring relationships, researchers found that many mentors struggled with mentees' cancellations, behavioral problems, and family difficulties, and generally felt overwhelmed by their mentees' social and emotional needs.[39] Through a series of in-depth postclosure interviews, researcher Renée Spencer and her colleagues found that nearly half of matches ended due to mentor abandonment, youth dissatisfaction, or gradual loss of momentum.[40] Mentors discussed feeling overwhelmed by mentees' complex needs and unprepared to address them. Several mentors felt unappreciated, unprepared for the difficult experience, and emotionally exhausted. As one mentor complained, "My expectation was, 'Gosh, I know a lot of young people who'd really appreciate me just calling them up! If I'm gonna do that for a young person I'm not related to, then it needs to be appreciated.'" Another mentor echoed this sentiment: "Obviously, when you volunteer, you're not expecting the world back. But you want something . . . you at least want to leave with a feeling . . . a good feeling." A third described the inherent complexities of mentoring a young person and the challenges of crossing class boundaries: "I just realized how very difficult it is to have any kind of intimate relationship. One-on-one relationships are hard and then with someone that is vulnerable like that . . . it's such a big responsibility." And a fourth noted, "It was hard to go over there . . . because I felt somewhat dismayed at their living situation. . . . [I] didn't know what I was gonna find. I was afraid."

These kinds of experiences can lead to burnout and mentor attrition. Across studies of teachers, youth service workers, counselors, and volunteers, work overload and role ambiguity (i.e., a lack of clarity over one's role and responsibilities) consistently predict burnout.[41] Without specific goals, some mentors may feel overwhelmed by a sense of obligation to "fix" everything.[42]

Mentoring program staff members, many of whom hold only a bachelor's degree (60 percent) or less (7 percent), can also experience overwork and burnout, which in turn reduce their capacity to support matches. In a recent national study of mentoring programs, 65 percent of staff members reported that frequent staff turnover is a significant concern for their agency, and only 42 percent agreed that their programs were adequately staffed to meet the needs of youth, whose referrals are often prompted by serious behavioral and mental health challenges.[43]

Given that formal mentoring programs tend to serve higher-risk youth, why have they generally been framed more in terms of light-touch recreation and friendship than as addressing therapeutic or other issues? The simplest answer may come down to a misclassification.

Misalignment with the Field of Positive Youth Development

The field of mentoring is often seen as an exemplar of positive youth development (PYD), an approach that emphasizes providing support and opportunities that build on youth's strengths. Specifically, as the mentoring movement was expanding in the late 1980s and early 1990s, psychologists were pushing for more empowering, less problem-focused views of youth. Two fields—positive youth development and prevention science—emerged concurrently from the recognition that many problems share similar risk (e.g., stress and trauma) and protective factors (e.g., extracurricular activities and caring adults).[44] Although both fields sought to strengthen protective factors, prevention scientists were more encompassing of risk factors, developing interventions that targeted those risks and stipulated guidelines for conducting program implementation and evaluation.[45]

The strengths-based focus of positive youth development grew both from valid arguments that young people should not be defined by their problems and early research showing that youth are more likely to thrive when their strengths are aligned with the resources and opportunities in their environments.[46] Although after-school, recreational, and other activity-based programs and settings (e.g., 4-H, Boys and Girls Clubs, Scouts, YMCA, and athletic leagues) fit naturally into this positive youth development framework, this was rarely the case for formal mentoring interventions. The latter tend to share far more in common with paraprofessional helping relationships and operate in ways somewhat detached from youth's broader contexts.[47]

I suspect that it was the focus on supportive, intergenerational relationships that led positive youth development programs to find common ground with formal mentoring programs. This focus helped to rationalize the field's alignment with positive youth development and the adoption of a more recreational approach. Although bound together by shared terminology, the relationships forged through mentoring programs (i.e., formal mentoring) are quite different from those that arise more organically (i.e., natural mentoring). Many natural mentoring relationships emerge in extended families, schools, and other settings where propinquity; obligations; and shared racial, ethnic, and cultural identities are potent drivers of enduring, committed intergenerational bonds. Nonkin natural mentorships might arise in schools, neighborhoods, positive youth development programs, and other situations where shared interests, regular contact, luck, and chemistry all play a part. Such relationships are not developed in response to any particular program or funding prerogatives, logic models, or time frames. The same cannot be said of formal mentoring programs, which share far more in common with the structures and imperatives of professional helping interventions. Relationships in formal mentoring programs are relatively short-term (e.g., only around 5.8 months on average in school-based mentoring) and, although they occasionally take on the contours of natural mentoring, this is not the norm. Granted, formal mentors sometimes meet with their mentees in after-school and other positive youth development settings, but that does not make the setting a mentoring program any more than meeting at Starbucks makes the coffee shop a mentoring program. Likewise, strong connections between youth and staff may arise naturally in after-school and other positive youth development programs, but that does not make those settings formal youth mentoring programs. In fact, youth's connections with staff in positive youth development programs tend to be distributed across several adults. In one ethnographic study of natural mentoring relationships in after-school programs, researchers observed that groups of staff members engage in "collective mentoring," where they share the responsibility to cultivate students' strengths and talents.[48] Youth similarly tend to distribute their natural mentoring needs across many adults. For example, one study found that youth can have as many as five natural mentors at a time, each filling different roles and needs.[49]

Whatever the reasons, the placement of mentoring programs under the umbrella of positive youth development has had major implications for the precision and rigor with which programs were developed. Since a major focus of positive youth development was on creating *settings* that were developmentally aligned with, and responsive to, youth's diverse strengths and interests, the field developed "without emphasis on specific intervention techniques or prescribed dosage and methods."[50] Positive youth development researchers instead documented settings' organizational features, opportunities, and relational processes, and their alignment with youth's interests and skills.[51] This worked for after-school and other programs, but was problematic for youth mentoring programs, whose constituents would have benefitted from targeted, evidence-based approaches. The light emphasis on risk, relative to activities and friendship, also meant that volunteer mentors were not always adequately trained to deal with the difficulties that so many young people were facing.

Researchers have argued that positive youth development's relatively imbalanced focus on promotion of positive outcomes rendered programs less effective than those that more fully encompassed risk and followed the norms of prevention science.[52] And, although positive youth development rests on a rich conceptual framework, the appropriation of its terminology by mentoring programs rarely included careful operationalization, implementation, and measurement of its core constructs.[53] Instead, mentoring programs largely drew on positive youth development's sunny, upbeat slogans, such as finding one's "spark," building "developmental relationships," and cultivating the "six Cs" (competence, confidence, connection, character, caring, and contribution) in ways that were inconsistently operationalized, and could not fully mitigate the multiple risk factors facing the youth the programs were serving.[54]

The construal of formal mentoring as more aligned with positive youth development programs also led to a focus on settings and strengths, and away from specific risks and vulnerability. Given this focus, few mentoring programs carefully tracked what their mentors were doing with their mentees or specified how particular activities would bring about particular outcomes. In fact, in its loose specification of activities, goals, and outcomes, as well as the overall absence of standardized evidence-based training of volunteers and youth, mentoring is something of an outlier in the broader field of volunteer interventions, largely eschewing the field's theoretical, evidentiary, and implementation standards.

Attempts have been made to bring greater precision into youth mentoring programs, and to incorporate monitoring, evaluation, and manuals that describe procedures. Yet the field has largely resisted such efforts.[55] It has also resisted efforts to move from omnibus, difficult-to-falsify conceptual models that explain how "mentoring works" toward a more precise specification of the conditions under which different approaches to mentoring might work for different youth. Psychologist Patrick Tolan and his colleagues have argued that the mentoring field's resistance to identifying, implementing, and adhering to standards, including specifying how inputs relate to outcomes, stems from its firmly held belief that the benefits of mentoring interventions flow mainly from close, enduring relational bonds.[56] Tolan and his coauthors note that, for youth mentoring, "the body of research is remarkable in the limited emphasis on systematic description of intervention content, description of intended processes through which effects are expected, and in important features of implementation and providers. There seems to remain limited commitment and perhaps even some reluctance to aim for continuity across the field or specificity in applying and describing mentoring efforts that might facilitate scientific understanding of effects."[57] Yet it is only through this sort of conceptual rigor that the field will reach its true potential.

Another team of researchers, led by psychologists Sam McQuillin and Michael Lyons, has also bemoaned the lack of specificity in how activities relate to outcomes in youth mentoring. They recently identified "a large discrepancy in how [mentoring] treatments are specified compared to other volunteer interventions."[58] In a review of fifty-seven published school-based mentoring program evaluations, McQuillin and his coauthors found that fewer than half of the studies even discussed the activities that occurred between mentors and mentees, with less than a quarter reporting either prescribed practices or guidelines for the meetings. Additionally, only 7 percent of the evaluations actually measured and reported the specific activities that mentors were expected to do with mentees. This absence of tracking "preclud[es] any legitimate understanding of what occurred between mentors and mentees" and contrasts with the extensive documentation of program content common to evaluations of other volunteer-based educational interventions.[59] Without information on what mentors and mentees actually do together, it is impossible to determine the extent to which programs are actually following recommended practices.[60] Nor is it possible to know what levers to pull to improve disappointing outcomes. One study found that those mentoring programs that monitor the way they are implemented obtain effect sizes three times larger than do programs that report no such monitoring.[61] Similarly, when researchers examined data from nearly five hundred studies across five meta-analyses of youth prevention programs, they found that effect sizes were double and sometimes triple the average when programs were carefully implemented.[62] Mentoring programs do not necessarily have to follow guidelines to the letter; research on social programs suggests that implementation can diverge and be customized as much as 40 percent from overarching guidelines and still achieve intended outcomes.[63] However, making such determinations requires that programs specify and measure what they are doing in the first place.

Taken together, a collective underestimation of risk and related overemphasis on strengths led the field of youth mentoring down a path of imprecise models that produce relatively weak effects. I will now describe the ways in which cognitive biases and miscommunication keep us on this path, rendering the field somewhat immune to counternarratives.

Cognitive Biases

A range of cognitive biases, particularly those stemming from the human preference for storytelling over data, have fueled the expectation that formal mentoring can routinely take on the characteristics of transformative natural mentoring. Isolated success stories tend to overshadow data showing that, on average, stronger effects generally emerge through targeted, evidence-based approaches. The allure of these stories is strong and can be explained, in part, by the "identified victim effect." This effect was first observed about a half century ago by economist Thomas Schelling, who stated, "Let a six-year-old girl with brown hair need thousands of dollars for an operation that will prolong her life until Christmas, and the post office will be swamped with nickels and dimes to save her. But let it be reported that without a sales tax the hospital facilities of Massachusetts will deteriorate and cause a barely perceptible increase in preventable deaths—not many will drop a tear or reach for their checkbooks."[64] This tendency to be moved more by singular examples than by the aggregate is particularly strong in youth mentoring programs and is the stock-in-trade of many fundraising efforts.

Poignant stories that trigger empathic responses also mute skepticism, even as the disappointing data pile up. However irrational, we instinctively react more strongly to the tug of a good story than to rafts of data suggesting how our money might be better spent. For example, in one study of donor responses to childhood poverty, people were asked to donate money to help a seven-year-old girl from Mali named Rokia. Many were so moved by Rokia's story that they gave generously. But when another group was told the same story about Rokia along with statistics about the scope and effects of poverty in Africa, they were *less* inclined to give. This and other studies have demonstrated that statistics are not only less persuasive but they appear to dampen generosity and compassion.[65]

Psychologist Paul Bloom implicates empathy in this tendency to focus on individuals over broader trends.[66] Empathy requires a laser focus on the individual; it competes with empirical analysis and the evaluation of broader solutions. When we shift our attention from one child to data on multiple children, we pull back and become more dispassionate.[67] This may have something to do with the fact that our brains evolved to have both a more emotional, experiential, automatic cognitive system, which is encoded in images and narratives, and a slower, more rational and analytic system that helps us make more deliberate decisions.[68] The former system enables us to instinctively jump away from the poisonous snake long before the latter can ever register a plan. The emotional system responded to the immediate dangers present in early human evolution; it did not develop to instinctively respond to or assess more distant problems like those conveyed in statistics. More generally, the dual process theory of cognition posits two systems that govern our decision making—an intuitive system that is quick, prone to error, and embedded in habitual patterns of behavior, and a second system that is systematic and slow but, when effectively harnessed, can correct or override the first system. Stories tend to evoke the more intuitive system and, as cognitive psychologist Vera Tobin observed, "the more emotionally engaged, the more gripping and vivid the story is, the less attention we're paying to the apparatus of this story and questioning and wondering and being on guard and monitoring these questions about, should I trust this source? What are the discrepancies here and so on? You're just immersed in that perspective."[69]

This tendency to get drawn into stories runs deep in the field of mentoring. Intellectually, we may know that the amazing young person and mentor standing at the podium during the gala are outliers—the mentoring equivalent of a Facebook photo of the perfect family on the perfect vacation—but emotionally we feel the tug. Somewhere in the back of our minds, a worried analyst might be wringing her hands, trying to break through with reminders about modest effect sizes, but that narrative is muted when a mentee with an inspirational story takes the stage.

The persistence of the less effective, nonspecific model can also be explained by gaps in communication between researchers and practitioners, and the open market of conflicting ideas about "what works" in mentoring. Several organizations have taken up the challenge of making accurate information about mentoring and other youth programs available through rating systems and reviews. The problem is that these groups tend to proceed independently, and because they do not always agree on the standards, their verdicts about effectiveness can vary greatly. When one set of findings about a program's effectiveness contradicts an earlier conclusion, the field's "best practices" in mentoring can suddenly seem up for grabs. This diversity of opinions can confound even the most committed practitioner or parent. Reflecting on this state of affairs in the broader field of youth interventions, researchers have argued for "a more unified system for reviewing the evidence for youth interventions and external reviews that move beyond the claims of the intervention developers and proponents."[70]

Yet even if the field were to adopt and implement a unified system, it would be hard-pressed to compete with the misleading, bias-confirming findings perpetuated at mentoring conferences, in promotional materials, and on websites. Simplified, upbeat, and visually appealing research summaries and infographics offer stiff competition to more rigorous evaluations, which rarely provide clear and simple answers that mentoring programs are looking to share with their funders. Given this mayhem, it is easy to see why practitioners fall back on belief-confirming anecdotes and success stories from their own programs as evidence of positive outcomes.

Psychologists Carol Tavris and Elliot Aronson have argued that this tendency to look for evidence of what we hold to be true is particularly strong in the field of helping relationships. They describe this as the "problem of the benevolent dolphin." They explain:

> Every once in a while, a news story appears about a shipwrecked sailor who, on the verge of drowning, is nudged to safety by a dolphin. . . . It is tempting to conclude that dolphins must really like human beings, enough to save us from drowning. But wait—are dolphins aware that humans don't swim as well as they do? Are they actually intending to be helpful? To answer that question, we would need to know how many shipwrecked sailors have been gently nudged further out to sea by dolphins, there to drown and never be heard from again. We don't know about those cases because the swimmers don't live to tell us about their evil-dolphin experiences. If we had that information, we might conclude that dolphins are neither benevolent nor evil; they are just being playful.[71]

Tavris and Aronson argue that psychotherapists can leap to "benevolent dolphin" conclusions, when, in the absence of experimental studies, they summon up "evidence" that their clients are improving and that their approaches are working. In much the same way, the field of mentoring has suffered from the flawed reasoning behind the benevolent dolphin problem.

The equity bias, which is the tendency to weigh all opinions (and by extension research findings) as equally valid, irrespective of the opinion holder's or program developer's expertise, also affects how we evaluate evidence. This bias runs deep in mentoring and cuts both ways—people with less expertise often think they know as much as everyone else, while experts tend to rate themselves on par with everyone else.[72] Moreover, nonexperts tend to have a bias favoring their own opinion, even when they might benefit from following more informed advice. In one study, a team of cognitive psychologists found that people assigned nearly equal weight to their own opinions and those of experts.[73] This tendency persisted even after participants were told about the expertise gap and even when they had a monetary incentive to maximize collective accuracy. The equity bias complicates decisions about how best to help young people. This overconfidence in personal expertise is particularly rampant in mentoring, where the familiar, easy-to-visualize concept of a helping relationship leads well-meaning mentoring funders to equate their success in other arenas (e.g., technology, finance, sports, or politics) with their likely success in what seems on the surface to be a pretty surefire and straightforward approach to helping youth.

Researcher-Practitioner Communication Gaps

An additional factor contributing to the persistence of the nonspecific youth mentoring model is the fact that researchers, practitioners, and policymakers tend to define key terms—"research" and "evidence"—quite differently. Whereas many researchers employ the two terms interchangeably to mean "findings derived from scientific methods," studies suggest that practitioners working in the field tend to define evidence more broadly as stemming not only from scientific methods, but also from consumer satisfaction surveys; feedback from parents, youth, and communities; and other sources.[74]

Practitioners' embrace of less-rigorous evaluations may stem in part from understandable frustration with researchers' seemingly slow and ponderous pace. Researchers' tendency to poke and prod at topics that can seem arcane and irrelevant can frustrate practitioners who have pressing concerns. Furthermore, scientific communications can be inscrutable and riddled with caveats, nuances, and frustrating ambiguities. Anyone who has ever endured a research presentation is familiar with such equivocation. It is the messy context that gives data meaning, but it is easy to see how a litany of qualifiers can come at the expense of being helpful to practitioners working in youth intervention programs. Efforts to be completely transparent about study limitations can seed doubt and misinterpretation about the findings.

Add to these communication gaps the growing antipathy toward evidence and, in the era of accusations about "fake news," a suspicion that experts may have a hidden agenda that leads them to play fast and loose with their statistics. Fewer than 20 percent of respondents in one large survey indicated that they trusted scientists in general, and statistics, in particular, appear to draw skepticism.[75] Sociologist William Davies notes that "not only are statistics viewed by many as untrustworthy, there appears to be something almost insulting or arrogant about them.... People assume that the numbers are manipulated and dislike the elitism of resorting to quantitative evidence."[76] Particularly in the context of what Davies describes as the "declining authority of statistics—and the experts who analyse them," many consumers of mentoring research may weigh a tally of responses from a nonrepresentative sample equally with the statistical analyses of a randomized clinical trial.

Then there's the glacial time frame for getting evaluation and research findings through the peer review process, into scholarly journals, and, eventually, into the field for uptake in practice guidelines for real-world settings. Given how byzantine this process can seem, and how little the public actually distinguishes between trainings and interventions that are peer-reviewed and those that are not, the temptation is strong for programs to skip the middleman and begin disseminating untested trainings and curricula. To an untrained eye, a finding is a finding, and the distinctions about evaluation designs and peer review are, let's just say, academic.

It can also be difficult to create and sustain a flow of new ideas between academia and practitioners.[77] Fortunately, there are plenty of innovative on-the-ground ideas that could inform science if they were tested through research collaborations.[78] For example, the program Becoming a Man (BAM) offers a strong model of the benefits of a two-way street and what such collaborations could look like. BAM was started by Chicago resident Anthony DiVittorio, who grew up on Chicago's South Side and obtained a master's degree in counseling psychology. Drawing on his personal and clinical experiences, DiVittorio developed BAM in partnership with other youth practitioners. After developing and refining the program for several years, DiVittorio worked with researchers at the University of Chicago, who evaluated BAM in randomized control trials. They found moderate to large effect sizes in reducing the likelihood of arrests in general, as well as a reduction in violent crime arrests specifically, and increases in school engagement and graduation rates.[79] BAM has since expanded and has developed a sister program, Working on Womanhood (WOW). These and other efforts (e.g., Harvard's Center on the Developing Child) pool the resources of practitioners and researchers and create a positive feedback loop that can hasten the adoption of evidence-based services by the field of mentoring.[80]

Thus far, I have laid out both the good and disappointing news about youth mentoring. This includes both the growing research evidence demonstrating the benefits of targeted interventions as well as the field's resistance to capitalizing on scientific advances.

I have also discussed the many possible reasons for this resistance, including confirmation biases that sustain unrealistic beliefs and a deep ambivalence about the role of research in guiding the terms of relationship-based interventions, and falsely dichotomous thinking about the relative merits of relationships versus targeted goals.[81] In the chapters ahead, I outline specific steps that programs can take to improve practice and to become more central players in addressing the wide gaps in the access youth have to effective care. Medicine, clinical psychology, and other fields have reaped benefits when they embraced effective practice. Youth mentoring is poised to follow a similar course. In doing so, the field will be better positioned to bridge service gaps and ensure that a larger fraction of vulnerable youth get the care and support they need.

4

GIVING PSYCHOLOGY AWAY

More than fifty years ago, community psychologist George Albee pointed to the wide and unbridgeable gaps between the small number of highly trained mental health professionals and the vast number of people who need care and support. He called for new models in which psychologists and other helping professionals move from providing direct service to supporting frontline lay providers:

> Let me emphasize, I do not see psychology as the care-delivery field. We can never have the manpower to meet the demands. Rather, we must create the theory, and show how it is applicable, to enable care to be given by bachelor's level people.... Psychology can only be the developer of the conceptual models and of the research underpinning.[1]

American Psychological Association president George Miller echoed this sentiment the following year in his presidential address, arguing that professionals' responsibility is less to "try to apply psychology ourselves, than to give it away to the people who really need it.... I can imagine nothing we could do that would be more relevant to human welfare, and nothing that could pose a greater challenge to the next generation of psychologists, than to discover how best to give psychology away."[2] He made this rallying cry amid the growing calls of community psychologists to expand mental health services by offering affordable clinics in neighborhoods and by empowering affected individuals and their communities to create their own solutions.[3] Innovative ideas—from developing mutual support groups to training bartenders, beauticians, and cab drivers in therapeutic techniques—were tested by community psychologists who saw the potential of lay providers on the continuum of care, recognizing that they were able to provide help that was comparable, and in some cases even preferable, to that of experts.[4]

Curiously, mentoring programs never really registered these clarion calls. Although they were essentially providing quasi-therapeutic care, volunteer mentors were rarely thought of as para-professionals (i.e., non-expert paid or volunteer care providers) or even as sitting on the same continuum of therapeutic care. The fact remains, however, that volunteer mentoring relationships and therapeutic relationships share much in common. For example, they are typically situated somewhat outside of the youth's network of family, friends, and community, and involve weekly "sessions." They are both characterized by inherent power differentials and a focus on only one member's improvement.[5] Mentoring also adheres to the same rituals as therapeutic relationships. In their classic book *Persuasion and Healing*, psychiatrists Jerome and Julia Frank noted that all helping relationships have four factors in common: a "confiding relationship with a helper," who "genuinely cares about their welfare, and has no ulterior motives"; a "healing setting," or context that is somehow set apart by time or location; a "rationale, conceptual scheme, or myth that provides a plausible explanation" for whatever difficulties led the person to seek out a helping relationship; and, finally, a ritual or intervention that both parties believe will be an effective means of restoring health.[6] These "nonspecific" factors create positive expectations that can help bring about positive change. Since formal mentoring satisfies these conditions, it occupies a place in the pantheon of healing interventions. And, although rarely acknowledged and not particularly systematic, formal mentors frequently draw on a wide array of established therapeutic techniques. For example, as mentors encourage their mentees to think and act in more adaptive ways, they may draw on principles of cognitive behavioral therapy (CBT), which help young people develop the skills needed to effectively address many of the most common psychological problems. Providing mentors with more systematic guidance for applying such tools may serve the additional purpose of increasing their sense of self-efficacy in the relationship, which is related to program effectiveness and match length.[7] With targeted tools and training, volunteer mentors can help to bridge our society's widening gulf between those youth who need help and those who get it.

Moreover, although funders may prioritize other issues, such as school success, it is important to note that mental health struggles often precede academic, social, and career difficulties. When youth learn and develop behavioral and emotional regulation skills (e.g., self-awareness, social awareness, decision making, self-management, and relationship skills), they are better positioned to keep impulses in check and focus on schoolwork.[8] Such skills are vital to youth who have been exposed to toxic stress. Exposure to violence and stressors can trigger automatic fight-or-flight neural connections (or circuits), and these impulses are in opposition to the more intentional responses needed to ignore distractions, pay attention, and learn.

Decades of research have shown that, with the right training and support, paraprofessionals can deliver interventions just as effectively as professionals—if not more so—in ways that could help to bridge the substantial gaps in care. Less than a third of children and adolescents who need mental health and related care actually receive any services; most of the services they do receive are not empirically supported, and these rates are even lower in ethnic minority populations.[9] The fact is that, even if every professional who provided youth services worked around the clock, there would simply never be enough of them to meet the needs of today's youth. Most professional mental health workers earn graduate degrees and professional licenses that require several years of study and certification and their specialized services are in high demand.[10] Many youth-serving mental health facilities are at capacity and have long waiting lists, and annual rates of staff turnover in the child- and adolescent-serving mental health workforce exceed 50 percent.[11] These shortages, as well as both attitudinal issues (e.g., concerns about stigma, cultural insensitivity, and low treatment effectiveness) and structural issues (e.g., cost, transportation, time, and access) have created overwhelming barriers for many parents who are seeking professional care for their children.[12] Yet, left untreated, many of the early social, emotional, behavioral, and academic struggles that emerge in childhood and adolescence grow more complicated and difficult to resolve. One solution is for youth to first work with paraprofessionals and then step up to more intensive professional services as needed.

The idea of asking paraprofessionals and other lay helpers to support, extend, or even replace professional helpers is not new. A solid base of research points to both the positive outcomes and economic benefits of doing so. Forty years ago, community psychologist

Joseph Durlak conducted a meta-analysis of all published studies that compared the outcomes of experienced psychologists, psychiatrists, and social workers with the outcomes of paraprofessionals, who, at the time, were defined in much the same way we might characterize today's volunteer mentors—that is, as "nonexpert, minimally trained community volunteers, students, and helpers."[13] Durlak had come of scientific age as a clinical community psychologist; this field embraced volunteers as both a natural and scalable alternative to traditional mental health providers. Frustrated with the post-World War II "medical models" of treatment and influenced by the social movements of the 1960s and 1970s, he was convinced of the need for more community-oriented approaches to mental health care. His analysis of forty-two evaluations led to a provocative conclusion that supported his ideas: across the board, paraprofessionals were actually *more* effective than trained professionals in providing mental health services. As he concluded, "professionals do not possess demonstrably superior therapeutic skills, compared with paraprofessionals. Moreover, professional mental health education training and experience are not necessary prerequisites for an effective helping person."[14] As Durlak later concluded, "The average person who received help from a paraprofessional was better off at the end of therapy than 63% of persons who received help from professionals."[15] These counterintuitive findings were met with skepticism and calls for additional research, because they challenged basic assumptions about the value of extensive training.

Over the next five years, researchers were able to replicate Durlak's findings, even after controlling for the difficulty of the people with whom professionals were working and the rigor of the studies.[16] A subsequent meta-analysis in 1980, which included 475 studies, found no relationship between years of experience and client outcome.[17] Likewise, in a 1987 meta-analysis of 108 studies of child and adolescent helping relationships, psychologist John Weisz and his colleagues found that seasoned therapists, graduate-student therapists, and paraprofessional therapists showed no differences in effectiveness.[18] Weisz, who has devoted his career to "developing and testing strategies for implementing and sustaining evidence-based interventions within everyday clinical care and educational settings for children and adolescents," recognized the important role for paraprofessional helpers in the service continuum as a credible yet more accessible alternative for working with many families, helping to extend the reach of services to underserved communities.[19]

Taking stock of these comparisons of mental health providers, one researcher noted, "In most professions it would [be] ludicrous to compare a trained and an untrained person. It is hard to imagine a study comparing trained and untrained surgeons or trained and untrained electricians for that matter. Dead persons in the first instance or dead trainees in the second could be the unfortunate outcomes."[20] And yet when it came to helping relationships, it seemed that, under the right circumstances, trained volunteer mentors could effectively support people who lacked access to trained professionals.

And herein lies the critical caveat: the *right circumstances* included experienced paraprofessionals, targeted interventions, and ongoing training and supervision. First, experience mattered: in the aforementioned studies, the volunteers and helpers with more experience showed the strongest effects relative to the professionals. Second, targeted interventions were more effective. In Durlak's study, the most effective helpers were those whose efforts were focused on specific targeted problems (e.g., depression and health behaviors) and not more general, broad outcomes. Third, the level of supervision that paraprofessionals received mattered. Durlak cited a study by psychologist Averil Karlsruher, who found that unsupervised college students were completely ineffective in helping to redress the difficulties of elementary school children, whereas carefully supervised college students achieved successful results that were equal to those of trained professionals.[21] Many of the studies covered by Durlak's meta-analysis included paraprofessionals who had received fifteen or more hours of training. Taken together, these findings suggest that the most important variables accounting for their effectiveness in comparative studies may have been the judicious selection, careful training, and ongoing supervision of the helpers.[22]

The relative benefits may also have stemmed from the standardization of treatment, particularly relative to the more freewheeling approaches of the day. As Durlak presciently observed:

> Paraprofessional effectiveness in some studies may be due to the development of carefully standardized and systematic treatment programs.... In these programs, treatment consists of a programmed series of activities. The more intervention procedures that can be clearly described and sequentially ordered in a helping program, the easier it is for less trained personnel to administer the programs successfully.[23]

The paraprofessionals felt more comfortable and held higher expectations when they used standardized procedures which, in turn, may have helped to account for their effectiveness. Paraprofessionals' common sense and "real-world" solutions may have been appealing, but the stronger effects may have stemmed from their careful training and supervision.[24]

Evidence that well-trained paraprofessionals can achieve outcomes comparable to (if not better than) those of mental health professionals has continued to accrue over the years. In a 1995 meta-analysis, researchers evaluated the results of 150 studies of child and adolescent psychotherapy and found larger overall treatment effects for paraprofessionals.[25] The most common paraprofessionals were parents or teachers who had been trained in targeted, behavioral intervention approaches. Remarkably, paraprofessionals were more effective than either student therapists or fully trained professionals, who did not differ from each other in their level of effectiveness. But the researchers added an important caveat to this finding: "We must emphasize, however, that the beneficial effects produced by paraprofessionals and students in these studies followed training and supervision provided by professionals who had, in most cases, designed the procedures."[26] In another review of several studies, researchers found that, when taught to implement rigorously applied methods, paraprofessionals achieved effects comparable to those of professionals. Overall, however, their review studies noted the need for careful screening, training, and supervision by professionals.[27]

Subsequent studies have continued to highlight the value of deploying trained paraprofessionals to address mental health and other needs. In 2005, a comprehensive review of the literature confirmed that paraprofessionals successfully helped individuals with anxiety and depressive disorders.[28] More generally, paraprofessionals have also proven to be effective in treating a range of difficulties, including autism, ADHD, traumatic stress, substance use, and depression.[29] In one randomized controlled trial, for example, high school–educated lay workers proved to be just as effective (and sometimes more effective) than professionals in the delivery of routine care for depression.[30] A more recent meta-analysis of seventy-seven mental health prevention programs for college students showed similar trends.[31] Nearly two-thirds of the programs were delivered by paraprofessionals, including university staff, students, graduate trainees, and student peers. Once again, paraprofessionals delivered prevention programs with as much success as the fully trained mental health staff. Clearly, the work of professionals can be extended by students, volunteers, and others to help narrow the mental health service gap.

Durlak's early studies indicated that paraprofessionals may have been outshining the professionals not because they were inherently more empathic or skilled, but because they were more clearly defining, targeting, and structuring their helping activities, at least relative to the commonly used talk therapy treatments of the era, most of which lacked evidence or a skills-training component. The same holds true in more recent studies, in which paraprofessionals were closely supervised to ensure they followed structured, manual-guided treatments, whereas, in many cases, professionals had more latitude to improvise.[32] Thus, paraprofessionals' relative superiority may stem from the fact that they are typically tasked with addressing very specific targeted problems with active, skills-based approaches. This contrasts with the more intuitive, relationship-focused but less effective "usual care" approaches that have remained popular among many mental health professionals and the majority of youth mentoring programs over the years.

Implications for Taking a Paraprofessional Approach in Mentoring

Taken together, these studies suggest that engaging well-trained and supervised volunteers in delivering or supporting evidence-based care could provide the most cost-effective alternative to professional care. If the youth mentoring field adopted this approach, it could dramatically extend access to evidence-based care while freeing up professionals to supervise paraprofessionals and to work with more severe cases.[33]

This approach also capitalizes on the fact that many of today's volunteer youth mentors have a background in the helping professions, making them particularly well-suited for this paraprofessional role. A recent large-scale study of typical mentoring programs found that a third of the volunteers had a job or role for ten or more hours a week in a "helping profession," in which they helped others directly, including tutoring, nursing, counseling, teaching, and coaching.[34] This suggests that many mentors are already prepared to take on paraprofessional roles. In fact, one of the strongest results to emerge from decades of research is that volunteers with backgrounds in the helping and teaching professions are particularly effective in working with today's youth. A 2018 study of representative mentoring programs in the United States showed that youth derived more benefits when they were paired with mentors who had experience in helping roles (e.g., teachers, counselors, or social workers) as opposed to mentors with no such experience.[35] In particular, a mentor's helping background was a significant moderator of program effects, improving outcomes in conflict management, help-seeking, and problem-solving, as well as affect, emotional symptoms, and conduct problems. Two comprehensive meta-analyses, conducted in 2002 and 2018, drew similar conclusions, finding that programs that included a higher percentage of mentors with helping backgrounds produced relatively stronger effects.[36] Similarly, mentoring programs delivered by teachers have shown the highest return on investment.[37] Finally, a 2016 study found that volunteer mentors with previous involvement with youth in their communities were more successful than those with no involvement in working with children and adolescents from high-stress backgrounds.[38] Although these various studies were not designed to pinpoint the specific practices of subgroups, and the factors underlying helping professionals' relative advantages remain unclear, the findings seem to converge.

Of course, these findings and recommendations do not suggest that *only* those with relevant experience or helping backgrounds can be effective mentors. In fact, programs that provide volunteers with sufficient training have produced laudable effects.[39] But they do point to the merits of considering mentors' experiences and professional background alongside other relevant variables (e.g., geographical proximity, race, and interests), which are often taken into consideration when making matches. Just as the broader field of mental health moves toward a stepped-care model, the mentoring field should consider mentor experience and expertise on a continuum, reserving more seasoned volunteers for youth who need them most.

Regardless of mentors' experience, targeted evidence-based approaches will likely be most effective when interventions are easily accessible, brief, relatively simple to learn and deliver, and offer a promising return on investment across various outcomes.[40] For example, in a recent systematic review, researchers examined twenty-seven studies of psychological treatment effectiveness. All treatments were delivered by paraprofessional community health workers or peers who were trained in general relationship-building practices (e.g., active listening and empathy) and short-term (i.e., fewer than ten sessions) empirically supported intervention approaches. Moderate to strong effects (0.36–0.62) were found across a range of mental health outcomes.[41] The authors concluded, "Our findings strongly indicate the need to expand the orthodox definitions of who is considered a mental health-care provider, what constitutes a psychological treatment, and where treatments can be delivered. Our findings point to using relatively simpler treatment protocols as the basis for more widely disseminating empirically supported psychological treatments."[42]

Drawing on mentors to provide paraprofessional care could improve access to mental health services in underserved communities by delegating professional tasks to volunteer mentors who have fewer qualifications and less extensive training.[43] Youth would progress toward more highly trained professionals and intensive services only if these earlier steps proved ineffective.[44] A stepped model of supervision, in which highly trained professionals provide supervision and consultation to direct supervisors, who then support paraprofessionals, can also extend expertise in ways that can help to address unmet mental health needs, particularly in schools. The school counselors, nurses, and social workers are typically the first line of defense for children who are struggling emotionally. In fact, nearly all students who ever obtain mental health services receive them at school. American youth are twenty times more likely to receive their mental health care in schools than in mental health centers in their communities. Students attending schools with more guidance counselors and other mental health providers show better attendance rates and academic performance, in addition to lower rates of suspension and disciplinary and school safety incidents.[45]

Unfortunately, even as the presence of police officers has expanded, public schools, particularly those in poorer districts, are facing critical shortages of such professionals. An estimated 14 million American students attend schools with no nurses, counselors, or mental health staff.[46] Other schools have ratios of only one guidance counselor to nearly nine hundred students, despite data that suggest a 10 percent boost in college enrollment for every additional high school guidance counselor.[47] Guidance departments are finding that their investment in student mental health is cutting into their capacity to provide college and career counseling services.[48] Moreover, nearly 90 percent of US public schools do not meet the minimum recommended professional standard of one psychologist per 750 students and at least one counselor and one social worker per 250 students.[49] Volunteer mentors can support and extend the work of overburdened frontline professionals in schools and other settings, essentially serving as an early step on the ladder of care.

A stepped-care model also enables program staff to more directly recognize the many professional and personal benefits to volunteers. Volunteer mentoring is a challenging undertaking, leading many mentors to give up when their sacrifice of time and energy is not rewarded with strong relationships, positive youth outcomes, or some indicator of success. Programs that provide academic or career credentials can recognize mentors' training and service hours and sustain their commitment through the inevitable trials and tribulations of working with today's mentees. This might include finding ways for mentors to satisfy preprofessional training requirements through access to professional supervision and/or providing opportunities for mentors to earn college credit, continuing education units, certifications, letters of recommendation, digital badges, and other micro-credentials.[50]

Thus far, I have argued for volunteer mentors to serve as paraprofessionals on a broader continuum of care. This stepped-care model expands access to care, gives volunteers clearer goals, and frees up professionals to both share their expertise and focus on more critical cases.

In the chapters ahead, I describe how the field can achieve such goals through three approaches: specialized, embedded, and blended mentoring. Smaller *specialized mentoring* programs are well-poised to target specific subgroups (e.g., youth aging out of foster care and unaccompanied refugees), special risks (e.g., depression, anxiety, and peer rejection), and/or specific goals (e.g., STEM training and applying to college) and achieve powerful outcomes. Such programs are typically incubated in research labs and rely on carefully trained and supervised students and trainees. Because specialized programs have narrow goals, they can train their mentors on a discrete range of intervention approaches and are relieved of the pressure to be comprehensive.

Mentoring programs serving a wide range of youth lack this luxury. They rarely have access to the many targeted, empirically supported interventions that would be needed to address their mentees' varied needs and goals, and their volunteers cannot be expected to deliver such interventions with fidelity. Moreover, when they do specialize, such programs can only hit the mark with a subset of mentees. It is thus understandable that nonspecific programs have defaulted to the common denominator, lighter-touch friendship models that can essentially be delivered to all youth, irrespective of their particular issues.

Some programs have solved this specialization conundrum by dispatching their volunteers into classrooms and other settings to support the delivery of curricula or targeted skills training. In these *embedded mentoring* programs, volunteers play a supportive role, helping youth to practice and eventually master the concepts and skills that youth are already learning in their classrooms and through their therapeutic or other services. This model holds promise but requires a high level of community integration and logistical finesse.

Table 4.1

All programs:	Recruit, screen, and train mentors; supervise matches; act as a liaison with parents, caregivers, teachers, etc.; conduct assessment		
Specific program roles:	**Specialized mentoring**	**Embedded mentoring**	**Blended mentoring**
	Train mentors to deliver targeted, evidence-based interventions	Embed mentors insystems that provide targeted, evidence-based interventions	Train mentors to support targeted, technology-delivered interventions
Mentor roles:	Deliver intervention	Provide supportive accountability and supervise practice	

SPECIALIZED, EMBEDDED, AND BLENDED MODELS OF MENTORING: In small, targeted programs, mentors can deliver the intervention, while in larger, nonspecific programs mentors can engage their mentees in interventions delivered by professionals or by technology through supportive accountability and supervised practice.

A new, potentially more scalable solution to nonspecialized programs' inability to target their mentees' diverse needs is on the horizon. *Blended mentoring* models involve incorporating the growing array of evidence-based, technology-delivered interventions into relationship activities. Youth learn and practice targeted skills through youth-friendly apps, with mentors reinforcing this engagement (see Table 4.1). In both embedded and blended approaches, mentors encourage youth to complete lessons and activities (supportive accountability) and provide contexts for youth to practice new skills (supervised practice). Across all three of these approaches to mentoring (specialized, embedded, and blended) mentoring programs continue to play a vital role in developing and maintaining matches.

The models described in Chapters 5 and 6 can increase the likelihood that the specific needs and goals of youth are addressed with rigor. Training paraprofessional volunteers to deliver and / or support interventions, in turn, will free up highly trained professionals to work with youth who are facing more serious struggles. This emphasis on evidence-based training in no way diminishes the importance of the mentor-mentee relationship. Indeed, the success of all approaches rests on the foundation of a strong, collaborative relationship. Thus, in Chapter 7, I review decades of research on factors common to all successful adult-youth bonds so that programs can more consistently strike that delicate balance between building relationships and delivering targeted interventions.

5

SPECIALIZED MENTORING

Prevention scientists Tim Cavell and Chris Elledge have argued that the field of youth mentoring should move from the dominant "mentoring-as-relationship" model (i.e., the nonspecific friendship model), where the primary goal is for mentors to form bonds with their mentees, to a "mentoring-as-context" model, where targeted, prevention focused, goal-driven experiences take place within a helping relationship.[1] As proof of concept, Cavell and Elledge describe their school-based mentoring program for children who were bullied at school. Building on principles of behavioral psychology, mentors in this program built solid working relationships with their mentees and also helped them navigate interactions with peers in the complicated context of a school lunchroom.[2]

There are many other examples of this kind of specialized mentoring model in practice. In one program, students who were taught to regulate their emotions showed improvements in their math and English scores, life satisfaction, and school attendance.[3] Likewise, the Arches Transformative Mentoring program has achieved impressive results by deploying paid mentors from backgrounds similar to those of their mentees who were on probation (i.e., "credible messengers") to deliver and support an interactive journaling intervention based on cognitive-behavioral therapy principles. Relative to a comparison group, reconviction rates among Arches participants were a remarkable 69 percent lower after one year of probation and 57 percent lower two years later, with the largest improvements in participants under the age of eighteen. The evaluation also showed marked improvements in participants' self-perceptions and relationships.[4] Other successful programs have drawn on highly trained students to follow specific processes to deliver mental health interventions to children.[5] These and other "mentoring-as-context" programs often require extensive training and ongoing supervision. For example, the Cross-Age Mentoring Program (CAMP), which is designed to improve children's school and interpersonal connections, requires twelve hours of initial mentoring training and twenty-eight hours of ongoing training activities.[6] These and other "mentoring-as-context" programs indicate that, under the right conditions, mentors can effectively deliver targeted, evidence-based programs.

Specialized mentoring approaches recognize that not all youth need the same type of mentoring given their different risk profiles, needs, circumstances, interests, and goals. Thus, rather than attempt to construct a unifying theory to explain how mentoring "works" for all youth, specialized programs focus their efforts on developing psychologically precise interventions that pinpoint the exact thoughts, behaviors, and contexts that give rise to mentees' particular struggles. Such precision enables programs to set clear boundaries around their service models and to draw on evidence-based practices that are aligned with the targeted goals of the populations they are serving. Volunteers are often trained in specific skills-based techniques, such as applied relaxation for anxiety or behavioral activation for depression.

In addition to imparting skills, most specialized mentoring programs highlight the value of "amicable but not necessarily deep relationships between mentor and protégé."[7] Close, enduring ties may emerge, but this approach does not frame them as the sine qua non of effective mentoring. As Cavell and Elledge note, "dropping the requirement of a close, lasting bond does not mean losing that magic, it simply recognizes that such moments cannot be prescribed."[8] Likewise, success does not necessarily depend on creating enduring ties, so programs are freed from the constraints of the year-long commitments that are traditional in many youth mentoring programs.[9] The original push for long-lasting ties in youth mentoring came from studies that showed the potentially harmful effects of prematurely terminated relationships.[10] Recent work, however, suggests that these troubling findings may have been pointing to feelings of rejection that disappointed mentees may have felt rather than the universal need for long relationships. In fact, the past three comprehensive meta-analyses in the field have shown no effects for match length.[11] Interestingly, the 2018 study found that programs that had expectations for longer meeting times actually yielded *smaller* effect sizes.[12] Although more research is needed to understand this unexpected finding, it may point to the need for programs to establish realistic expectations around time commitment to keep mentors from terminating early.[13] As noted, many mentoring programs struggle with high rates of mentor turnover, and the constraints and interruptions of academic calendars can make it difficult for school-based programs to sustain momentum. Even in the best cases, most school-based relationships do not persist into a second academic year, and a fair share dissolve after just one semester.[14] These realities highlight the wisdom of creating opportunities for more manageable obligations that don't overtax the volunteer.[15] Psychologist Sam McQuillin guarded against excessive attrition by adjusting to the realities of student volunteers who, he determined, were only able to predictably commit to about an hour or two per week for three or four months. Students had the opportunity to continue, but they did so by making commitments for small chunks of time (Sam McQuillin, pers. comm., 2018). Overall, rather than prescribing universal time frames to all mentoring programs, it is best to determine the number and timing of meetings based on target populations, program goals, and the minimum amount of intervention needed to achieve those goals.

Many specialized mentoring programs are based on principles of prevention science, which provide guidance for implementation, evaluation, and dissemination. To this end, the National Implementation Research Network (NIRN) has led many prevention programs through the process of selecting and implementing evidence-based interventions. The NIRN website contains a database of tools and resources that help programs to specify underlying change processes and identify the best available interventions that would facilitate such change.

Many of the most successful specialized mentoring programs share several of the following features in common. They are usually developed and tested by researchers and implemented under carefully supervised conditions that ensure that mentors stick with the program. The mentors usually have some level of accountability (e.g., course credit, clinical hours, or compensation) that ensures their consistent level of engagement. The programs typically include intensive volunteer training and require demonstrated competency before mentors work with youth. For example, one highly effective specialized program requires new volunteer mentors to pass two sets of training performance tests, conduct a supervised dry run, and participate in online booster sessions and site visits to ensure implementation fidelity.[16] In another program, based on cognitive-behavioral principles, mentors received nearly twenty-four hours of initial training to increase adherence to the protocol as well as a half-hour of supervision per week.[17]

This approach to mentoring is not without its challenges. For instance, not every youth needs every aspect of a specialized, multi-component program. Also, some may present with several issues that defy a single approach. Although many problems confronting youth stem from similar factors, different youth may need a different balance of approaches. As mentoring experts Marc Wheeler, Thomas Keller, and David DuBois concluded, "Given the diversity of school-based mentoring models and programs and the fact that mentoring is an individualized intervention, planners must consider which model will work for which students under which circumstances."[18] Different mentees may require different components or combinations of approaches.

One solution to this need for more individualized care is to take a modular approach, which allows programs to select from a menu of evidence-based protocols based on the particular needs of a given youth.[19] In doing so, a modular approach enables more personalized interventions. By zeroing in on exactly what is needed, modular treatments have the potential to address several problems at once.[20] Dennis Embry and Anthony Biglan, for example, distilled fifty-two "behavioral kernels"—skills, knowledge, or behaviors such as problem-solving, coping with stress, and relaxation—that program staff can assemble and instruct mentors to implement depending on a youth's needs and circumstances.[21] For example, anxiety and depression often co-occur and frequently give rise to youth's behavioral struggles.[22] Modular treatment manuals that can target the underlying factors shared by the most common mental health problems (i.e., depression, anxiety, and stress responses) are more practical and responsive.[23] Having access to a menu of discrete intervention strategies enables programs to respond more nimbly to mentees' needs and circumstances.

Yet even the best of the specialized "mentoring-as-context" approaches remain elusive to most youth. What are the odds that a particular young person, struggling with a particular issue or set of issues at a particular time and place, will have access to a specialized, evidence-based mentoring program that meets his or her needs? Many of the most effective specialized approaches are implemented in settings that are proximal to the universities where they are developed and are launched in response to time-limited funding opportunities. Youth are much more likely to be referred by their parents or teachers to large, nonspecialized programs that may have rolling enrollment but neither the portfolio nor volunteers to deliver specialized evidence-based services with fidelity. Even if nonspecialized programs could identify the best approaches to working with every child who walks through their doors, and even if they could provide sufficient training and oversight to their volunteers, the current system of incentives would present hurdles. Many volunteer mentors already feel overwhelmed by the task of forging and sustaining a productive bond with their mentees. Asking them to invest additional time into learning and delivering specialized skills training programs may simply be a bridge too far.

This risk of overtaxing volunteers is a particularly salient issue for programs that rely on volunteers, as opposed to mentors who are students, trainees, or otherwise compensated. Such programs have little leverage over their volunteers, who can reschedule or even skip meetings with relative impunity. This, in turn, derails the sequence and momentum of targeted, evidence-based programs. If the success of mentoring interventions hinges on the willingness of uncompensated volunteers to consistently show up and deliver an intervention according to plans, we are baking a certain level of heartache into the enterprise. And if the volunteer drops out altogether, the entire intervention comes tumbling down—that is, unless a new volunteer mentor is quickly assigned to the abandoned youth, a practice that may be of questionable value.[24] Thus, although targeted, evidence-based approaches are most effective, large, nonspecialized programs are rarely structured to deliver them.

Interventions as Contexts for Mentoring

To hedge against such risks, I recommend solutions in which volunteers in larger, nonspecialized programs support, but do not necessarily deliver, targeted evidence-based interventions—in this case, the intervention becomes the context for mentoring. For example, programs can dispatch and embed their trained mentors within educational, mental health, and other systems where they can support and practice lessons and skills that are already being delivered (e.g., helping with math problems or practicing social and emotional learning skills). Looking to broader trends in the fields of health and mental health care, another promising approach may be for mentors to support mentees' use of targeted, evidence-based apps by encouraging engagement and providing opportunities for supervised practice. In both instances, the mentor's role shifts from delivering interventions to helping youth fully engage in the interventions they are receiving.

Mentors have a vitally important role to play in this regard, particularly as intervention programs move toward encouraging more active forms of skills training. Most effective cognitive and behavioral skills-training programs require multiple sessions, as well as opportunities for youth to practice, master, apply, and integrate each new skill.[25] Unfortunately, because many of these programs are pressed for time, relatively few can afford to set aside time for supervised practice sessions.[26] For example, nearly a quarter (22 percent) of the college mental health programs in a recent meta-analytic review included no opportunities for supervised practice.[27] Similarly, although between-session homework can extend the lessons in cognitive and behavioral skills-training programs, few require homework. Yet a meta-analysis of studies that compared interventions with and without between-session homework strongly favored the use of homework (0.48).[28] Providing supervised practice and monitoring in the context of such skills-training programs represents a clear, well-defined, and extremely promising role for mentors.

The Promise of Supervised Practice

Practice sessions with mentors can help mentees understand and generalize what they are learning in skills-training programs, as well as apply the skills to real-life situations. Although supervising youth as they practice new skills may seem like a trivial task, it can dramatically improve the effectiveness of programs (see Figure 5.1).[29] Compared to instruction-only skills modules, programs that provide young people with supervised opportunities to practice and to receive feedback on the skills and behaviors they are learning yield far stronger effects than those without the practice component. In one meta-analytic review of over one hundred universal prevention programs for young adults, for example, researchers found that those that included supervised practice in targeted, skills-based

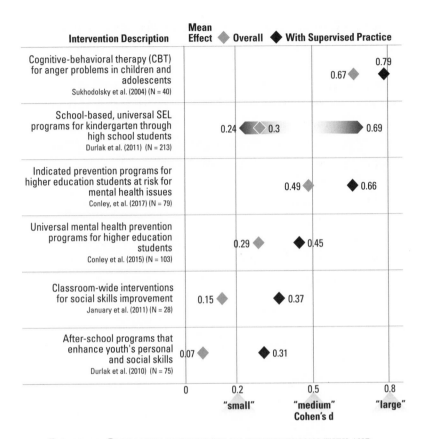

FIGURE 5.1: COMPARING THE EFFECTS OF INTERVENTIONS WITH AND WITHOUT SUPERVISED PRACTICE: Intervention effects improve when youth are given supervised opportunities to practice the skills that they are learning.

programs were significantly more effective than those that did not incorporate supervised practice.[30] The authors noted that "without supervised practice, it is highly unlikely that participants will be able to master new behaviors and apply them appropriately in the future."[31] Mentors are well-positioned to supervise their mentees as they learn, practice, and master important new skills.

In Chapter 6, I'll describe embedded and blended mentoring models that build on this logic. Rather than headline the mentoring show, mentors in these models play a supporting role, helping to ensure that the youth who participate in intervention programs remain fully engaged in the programs and willing to incorporate their new skills into their daily lives. If mentors miss a day or two, or drop out altogether, the show can still go on. But when they do show up, mentors can play a well-defined, catalyzing role that boosts the effectiveness of targeted, evidence-based interventions.

6

The Promise of Embedded and Blended Mentoring

Javier was just four years old when he immigrated to San Diego with his parents and younger brother to live with his aunt. His dad had been involved with the labor movement in El Salvador and was forced, by threat of violence, to flee to the United States. Although Javier had managed to secure a spot in one of the city's coveted dual-language learning classrooms, his struggles with reading English made it nearly impossible to learn in his new land. Fortunately for Javier, his school district partnered with Experience Corps, an organization that recruits, screens, trains, and then dispatches mentors to schools to work with struggling students like Javier.[1] Rather than students being pulled from class to meet with their mentors—a practice that can result in significantly lower math and language grades—mentors in the Experience Corps program sit through class alongside their mentees.[2] Then, during group time, the mentor works with the student to sound out and understand words. Teachers tend to appreciate this more targeted approach, which reinforces, rather than competes with, class content. The program's cofounder, John Gardner, envisioned Experience Corps in the 1990s as "operation give-back," a two-way street that could also provide older adults with a sense of meaning and purpose.[3] For older adults, such mentoring can provide a sense of accomplishment, offset feelings of stagnation and loss, and even delay or reverse declining brain functioning.[4] For children like Javier, this process can make all the difference.

Javier was matched with Eduardo, a retired naval officer who had become a dependable volunteer for Experience Corps. Over time, Eduardo also learned about Javier's traumatic immigration circumstances and was able to see the ways they continued to reverberate through his very sense of being. One day, when a nearby student dropped a stack of plastic lunch trays, Javier instinctively jumped into Eduardo's arms, a move that practically melted Eduardo's heart. Relationships like these can make a huge difference. An evaluation showed that students like Javier, who worked with Experience Corps' volunteers, scored 60 percent higher than those in control groups on both reading comprehension and sounding out new words.[5]

This model of embedding mentors into broader systems of support has also been successfully implemented in other settings.[6] Thread, a Baltimore-based program, dispatches volunteers to work with students who are performing in the bottom 25 percent of their class. According to *New York Times* writer Daniel Bornstein, Thread is "refreshingly realistic about the capacities of its volunteers and services and the systems-level issues facing their young people."[7] Instead of providing direct services, Thread partners with hundreds of service providers, deploying mentors to help connect and engage youth in these services. In another program, Fostering Healthy Futures, students in social work programs serve as mentors to youth who are aging out of foster care, attending workshops with their mentees and helping them practice the skills they are learning in therapy.[8] Many programs like these draw on trauma-informed cognitive-behavioral therapy, the gold standard for working with children and adolescents who suffer from post-traumatic stress disorder.[9] Professionals who deliver these and other skills-based interventions sometimes ask caregivers to practice and reinforce the skills learned in therapy, a job that is well-suited for paraprofessional mentors.[10] Similarly, therapeutic mentoring models, in which trained mentors are dispatched to outpatient mental health centers to serve as an "adjunct to therapy and a context to safely practice social and other skills and transfer them to their homes and communities," are being increasingly deployed.[11]

Mentors have also worked successfully within juvenile justice systems in this capacity. For example, Aftercare in Indiana through Mentoring (AIM) deployed mentors to help reinforce skills that youth were learning as they transitioned out of juvenile detention. Compared to youth who received only information, those who also received mentoring to help them through the re-entry process showed better outcomes, including significantly lower rates of later re-incarceration, arrests, and convictions.[12] Along similar lines, the National Guard Youth Challenge Program requires youth to recruit mentors who can help them practice and consolidate new skills as they move to and through an intensive residential program. A rigorous evaluation of this program highlighted the importance of mentors in sustaining the gains made by youth in the years following the program.[13]

Community schools offer another context for embedded mentoring. In community schools, a school coordinator typically conducts comprehensive assessments of all students' academic, social, emotional, physical, and psychological challenges and strengths, and then refers each student to specialized services such as cognitive behavior therapy, health care, food and housing assistance, and job training.[14] Community schools seek to work with children and families in a more holistic, interconnected way rather than through the more piecemeal approaches that typify many service systems. For example, in the Boston-based City Connects system, each community school has a site coordinator who conducts thorough assessments of students' strengths and needs. Students are placed in risk categories, with those at the highest level referred to a wider array of mental health care, medical care, and other services through the schools' multiple partnerships throughout the surrounding communities. Compared with peers who were never enrolled in a City Connects school, students achieve better reading, writing, and math grades in elementary school and do better on statewide math and English language arts tests in middle school.[15] Students who were enrolled in City Connects elementary schools later had better attendance and dropped out of high school at about half the rate of comparison students.[16]

A particularly valuable role for embedded mentors could be to support student involvement in the many social-emotional learning (SEL) classes that are being offered in schools. Social-emotional learning programs are designed to help youth learn and develop skills (e.g., self-awareness, social awareness, decision making, self-management, and relationship skills) to understand, recognize, manage, and express emotions; set goals; and develop positive, empathic relationships.[17] Such skills are vital to many youth who have been exposed to chronic stress (e.g., living in poverty or repeated exposure to violence). As mentioned in Chapter 4, these types of stressors often elicit autonomic fight-or-flight neural connections (or circuits) in the brain that crowd out the development of circuits that govern the intentional responses needed to pay attention and learn.[18] Mentors can help youth practice and apply emotional and behavioral regulation skills in daily life.[19]

Embedded mentors can also support parents and other caregivers who are asked to participate in parallel sessions as an adjunct to their children's treatment. Although caregiver involvement can boost and extend intervention effects, caregivers from marginalized and underserved backgrounds often face extensive financial, logistical, language, and other barriers to participation.[20] Some describe feeling blamed, misunderstood, or not heard by their children's teachers and therapists.[21] Yet, as psychologist Alicia January and her colleagues state, "If the social and emotional needs of children are going to be addressed more fully, the entire environment, home, school, and community must work together to create a supportive atmosphere that emphasizes the importance of social skills."[22] Particularly since marginalized caregivers are sometimes distrusting of mental health services, mentors can serve as a culturally trusted liaison across these contexts.

Finally, embedded mentors can increase youth's awareness of the resources available to them, encouraging them to trust other adults and to access resources. In their study of students at risk for dropping out of school, researchers have described how natural mentors can serve as "anchors" in the web of support that may already exist in marginalized students' schools and service settings. Embedded volunteer mentors can also serve as anchors. The researchers noted that trust in just one caring adult increased students' willingness to access and engage with other providers, stating that students "could be standing in a room full of support, but they need someone to turn on the lights so they can see what's there and reach for it."[23]

The embedded mentoring model also has economic benefits. Because practice expedites and improves youth's acquisition of skills, embedded mentoring can also help bridge service gaps by reducing the number of sessions necessary to achieve positive outcomes in professional care and by boosting those outcomes. Embedding mentoring into broader systems of care may also yield better returns on investment. A recent economic analysis of youth mentoring showed that the marginal cost of school-based mentoring programs is about one third less per enrollee than that of stand-alone community-based mentoring programs, which require additional recruitment efforts, staff time, and program resources.[24]

Overall, mentoring programs that dispatch their volunteers to schools and other settings can help to support and leverage the academic, cognitive-behavioral, social-emotional learning, and other skills that youth are already receiving, while serving as trusted liaisons that can help to engage youth and their caregivers more fully. Large, nonspecific mentoring programs have a long history of embedding students in schools to provide friendships, but this has typically been in the form of an additional service that is not integrated with students' classwork or services.

Although more promising, the embedded model may not be feasible on a grand scale. Integrating, coordinating, and dispatching large numbers of volunteers across multiple service systems and bureaucracies may simply prove too vexing. Fortunately, a more self-contained, technology-blended approach that enables mentors to support targeted, evidence-based interventions is right on the horizon: blended mentoring.

Blended Mentoring

If you own a smartphone, you have probably downloaded at least one application that has promised some form of self-improvement—

from losing a few pounds to mastering mindfulness. On its own, your app may not seem particularly consequential but, collectively, smartphone apps and other technology-delivered interventions are quietly revolutionizing behavioral health and mental health care. What's more, they might just transform youth mentoring. Mental health apps (MHapps), for example, can successfully address a range of common mental health concerns.[25] Apps can also be used to help youth achieve a range of academic and career goals, from applying to college to discovering new career paths. When technology-delivered interventions are blended with coaching and support in what is called blended mentoring, they can produce outcomes that rival those of face-to-face interventions, often at little or no cost and in ways that are more geographically, financially, and socially acceptable to youth and their caregivers.[26]

Despite this promise, youth and adults alike struggle to remain engaged in self-administered apps, and as many as three-quarters don't complete the recommended number of sessions.[27] Compared to self-guided apps, those that incorporate some form of coaching to help users remain actively engaged are far more effective.[28] So, in a nutshell, we have targeted, evidence-based apps that work best for youth when they are supported by lay coaches; and we have mentoring programs that are in need of targeted, evidence-based interventions. This may just be a match made in heaven. Here's why.

First, the ubiquity of smartphones and the development of mobile mental health, health, and wellness apps have made evidence-based care accessible in ways that could shift the mentoring landscape. Many incorporate engaging, intrinsically motivating interactive lessons, quizzes, games, and virtual rewards, and 95 percent of young people already have access to smartphones and are in the habit of checking them many times a day.[29] Youth also appreciate the autonomy and reduced stigma that MHapps can afford, and many prefer to handle their issues on their own.[30] Additionally, the best MHapps are digital applications of cognitive behavioral therapy principles, including methods to cope with stress, and techniques such as journaling or tracking thoughts, feelings, and behaviors. This sort of self-monitoring can also help young people recognize, label, and ultimately better regulate their emotions.[31]

Some apps have incorporated coaching dashboards that could enable mentors to easily track, encourage, nudge, and reward mentees' engagement. These dashboards can also facilitate program staff efforts to monitor matches. Additionally, many apps have incorporated sophisticated data collection techniques (e.g., time sampling youth's moods, conducting randomized assessments, automatic scoring, and visualization of data) which, aided by machine learning, can simplify, expedite, and improve the capacity of programs to monitor and evaluate their efforts.[32] Increasing the frequency, accuracy, and efficiency of data collection and analysis has potentially far-reaching effects (e.g., enabling early detection of problems and more targeted support as well as reducing the need for costly program evaluations). Apps are also able to address the needs of underserved and marginalized groups, who tend to rely on their smartphones even more heavily than do their more privileged counterparts and have less access to in-person programs. Some evidence-based apps have been adopted for use across racial and ethnic groups, helping to spread linguistically and culturally acceptable interventions while reducing waitlists in overburdened mental health systems.[33] Likewise, many app-based interventions can be completed in a matter of months or even weeks, potentially releasing volunteers from the traditional one-year mentoring commitment so they can work with additional youth. Mentees on waitlists may also benefit. Frontline staff can draw on youth's intake data to recommend targeted, evidence-based apps for waitlisted youth to work on with family members or other caring adults.

In addition to improving access to care, apps have reduced financial barriers. Although some require fees and subscriptions, a growing number of federally funded behavioral health and MHapps are publicly available at little or no cost. Built on years of research and evaluation, they can also readily incorporate new research and practice updates as their fields advance. For example, Northwestern University's Center for Behavioral Intervention Technologies offers an array of health and mental health apps that cover depression and anxiety, thoughts and feelings, activities and emotions, social support, and more. When paired with coaching, these apps have produced significant improvements in health and anxiety in as little as eight weeks.[34] Along similar lines, mindfulness and meditation apps have shown positive effects on users' depressive symptoms and school adjustment, irritability, mood, and stress management.[35] Some MHapps are being developed and adopted with youth programs in mind since the marginal costs of scaling to new users and/or reusing the training again and again are trivial. For example, SuperBetter was designed to "help youth-focused organizations increase resilience, promote social and emotional learning, and reduce student anxiety and depression," and has shown impressive effects on youth depression levels.[36] Apps are poised to extend the reach of evidence-based care to more youth.

Unfortunately, the potential to do so, particularly for MHapps, has been limited by low engagement, improper use, and high rates of noncompletion in the absence of coaching and support.[37] Engaging youth in mental health services has always been a challenge, and self-administered MHapps are no exception. Compared to the rates of other health and wellness apps, MHapps have the lowest use after one month, even when mental health care providers recommended them.[38] The most common solution to these difficulties has been to provide users with coaches who can help boost engagement through what behavioral scientists refer to as "supportive accountability"—that is, regular check-ins, monitoring, troubleshooting, and other interactions. Supportive accountability seeks to isolate and efficiently address common difficulties or "failure points" that are often encountered in app-based interventions. These include usability (design flaws in the app), user engagement (a lack of motivation), fit (the app does not address the user's specific needs), knowledge (incorrectly using the app), and implementation (insufficient incorporation of new skills into the user's daily life).[39] Supportive accountability coaches seek to identify the failure points and maintain engagement with the app, not deliver the actual intervention.

Several studies and systematic reviews have highlighted the positive associations between supportive accountability and users' engagement, number of logins, use of interactive tools, and outcomes.[40] These studies have shown that, with guidance, effect sizes of apps and other technology-delivered interventions are comparable to those obtained in face-to-face interventions, whereas entirely self-guided programs have yielded relatively few benefits.[41] A recent large-scale meta-analysis, for example, showed that students whose use of technology-delivered interventions was supported by coaches, either in person or through online contact, showed more gains than those who self-administered their interventions.[42] In fact, supported interventions produced nearly double the effects of self-administered interventions (0.55 versus 0.28). As the researchers noted, "support from paraprofessionals or even peers might enhance participant goal setting, expectations, and motivation, and thus improve intervention engagement, adherence, and outcomes."[43]

In a recent meta-analysis of sixty-six randomized control trials of MHapp interventions, researchers found that studies that offered guidance (e.g., regular supportive text messages, phone calls, and personalized feedback) and engagement reminders yielded effects that were more than double those of studies in which no such support was provided (e.g., 0.51 versus 0.21 for anxiety; 0.48 versus 0.23 for depression). Even simple reminders dramatically increased the effects of app-based interventions (0.15 versus 0.39 for anxiety; 0.18 versus 0.32 for depression).

Importantly, this coaching and support need not be delivered by highly trained professionals. Previous studies have found no difference in technology-delivered engagement or outcomes when youth were supported by clinicians versus nonprofessionals.[44] Supportive accountability need not be delivered in person and requires relatively little time on the part of the coach or mentor. Clearly, there is a role for mentors in providing such reminders and guidance.

The science of supportive accountability is still new and needs testing and refinement with youth mentors.[45] Careful prospective studies on the effects of supplementing mentoring relationships with MHapps, for example, are needed to understand their effects and to ensure that any potential benefits are not offset by unintended consequences. We will need to study their feasibility across different geographical, socioeconomic, age, and racial/ethnic groups. Other issues, including cultural sensitivity, intergenerational technology gaps, privacy, and ethical concerns, will need to be resolved as targeted, technology-delivered interventions are blended with mentoring practice.[46]

Mentor training will also need to be updated to incorporate the lessons of supportive accountability. For example, research on MHapps suggests that support is most effective when coaches are clear about goals from the start; monitoring and check-ins are framed as helpful (and not controlling); and the coach is perceived as trustworthy, benevolent, and having the necessary expertise. Likewise, MHapp users respond better to low-intensity accountability; efforts to engage the user beyond a certain threshold may be counterproductive.[47] Research also suggests that supportive accountability is most effective when expectations are focused on the process (i.e., gaining mastery) as opposed to simple adherence, as the latter can lead to more perfunctory engagement.[48] For this reason, supervised practice may be needed to ensure that youth learn and master new skills.[49]

As the field embraces technology-delivered interventions, we must keep in mind that the universe of apps is continuously expanding and very few apps have associated scientific evidence.[50] There are possible risks associated with app-based smartphone interventions, including the ease with which youth may access potentially ineffective or even harmful interventions. Resources like PsyberGuide.org have simplified the process of selecting appropriate, evidence-based apps that may offer a viable solution to nonspecific youth mentoring programs, helping to bridge the gaps in service. As the authors of a recent meta-analysis of MHapps concluded, "smartphone interventions could eventually serve as a low-cost, easily accessible, and user-friendly option for universal, selective or indicated preventive programs. Smartphone interventions could also fit within the stepped-care model, in which low intensity interventions are offered as a first step in treatment, with more intensive resources reserved for those who fail to respond."[51]

In blended mentoring models, volunteers could provide supportive accountability through the app throughout the week. They could then devote some portion of the in-person meetings to supervised practice to ensure that youth are using, integrating, and personalizing the new skills and concepts. The remainder of the meeting could be used for conversations and fun activities that help to build and maintain good working relationships.[52]

In fact, across all of these models, a focus on incorporating effective intervention models in no way diminishes the importance of good working relationships, which provide the necessary motivation and support for youth's engagement and learning. Decades of clinical research have highlighted the independent contribution of nonspecific or "common factors," such as a therapist's warmth and empathy, as an essential foundation for delivering any effective care.[53] It is thus surprising that the field of mentoring has not directly harnessed clinical research on building strong alliances with children and adolescents.[54] Clinical studies have highlighted, for example, the importance of psychotherapists' sensitivity and interpersonal skills, including their verbal fluency and warmth.[55] Likewise, mentoring researchers have pointed to the importance of mentor sensitivity and attunement, as well as the actions that give rise to difficulties and failure. For example, after conducting in-depth studies of mentoring ties, mentoring expert Renée Spencer conceded that perhaps not every volunteer has the capacity to be a mentor: "The commonly held belief that virtually anyone can be a mentor may not in fact be quite true, and more attention needs to be paid in research and practice to determine what it takes to meaningfully engage a young person in the mentoring process."[56] To this end, Chapter 7 provides a brief summary of scientific literature on factors that are common to all effective therapeutic relationships.

7

The Good Enough Mentor

An unexpected phone call was the turning point in Molly's relationship with her seventeen-year-old mentee, Alana. During their first meeting, Alana reminded Molly of a skittish deer, and in each subsequent meeting Alana seemed to waver between seeming indifference and ever-so-slight engagement. Alana had grown adept at forcing relationships to their breaking point, thereby confirming her initial suspicions that adults could not be trusted. Undaunted by this protective posturing, Molly persisted, intuiting that deep down, Alana had an aching need for connection.

Molly's patience was rewarded that afternoon when a tentative Alana phoned her at work, asking if she had a minute to talk. "And this was a huge step because it was the first time that she had called. . . . I was juggling all kinds of things and immediately, I was like 'Absolutely!' I just decided that I needed to drop everything at that moment because it meant so much to me that Alana had reached out. And I was gonna make it happen, you know?" Molly's unflinching response was spot-on; a gossamer thread had been thrown her way and she was intent on catching it. Molly instinctively knew that Alana would sniff out even the slightest hint of hesitation. Instead, her warm, matter-of-fact response was pitch-perfect. Molly worked through the angles of Alana's difficult encounter with a teacher that day, ultimately paving the way toward a stronger connection and Alana's deeper commitment to the broader goals of their mentoring program.

Relationship expert John Gottman has observed that in any interaction, there are countless ways, both verbal and nonverbal, that people let their needs be known. They do this by making "bids" for connection: "They are asking for attention, interest, conversation, humor, affection, warmth, assistance, support and so on."[1] Mentors' attunement to these bids can make or break a relationship.[2] More generally, psychologists often talk about developing and maintaining strong relationships in terms of a "working alliance." An alliance or partnership is thought to consist of related components, including a warm bond, agreement on the goals, and an agreement on the strategies for reaching these goals.[3] Although evidence for strong working alliances is correlational, studies have highlighted their importance.[4] Researchers have identified a range of helping behaviors, or "common factors," that seem to foster strong alliances, including positive regard, expressing empathy, and fostering a sense of collaboration.[5] These and related findings, which highlight the importance of a strong alliance, are helping to settle the falsely dichotomous "either-or" debates about the relative contribution of relationships versus targeted, evidence-based approaches to youth mentoring. In some cases (e.g., when youth have insecure attachments), the very process of gaining trust and building an alliance may be therapeutic in its own right.[6] Additionally, for youth who may lack caring adult support in their daily lives, a strong bond with a volunteer mentor can make an enormous difference in their sense of self and identity. But programs cannot bank on close, transformative bonds as a matter of course. There will always be extraordinary relationships that deepen over time, but all mentors should be well prepared to build and maintain a working alliance that is sufficiently strong that youth remain engaged in the tasks at hand. In other words, alliance-building and skill-building are two sides of the same coin.

Good Enough Is Good Enough

A good working relationship is a necessary ingredient of all successful mentoring. It can provide a safe, supportive foundation for learning new skills and navigating challenging topics and tasks. In one mentoring program, for example, high school seniors who had expressed an interest in college but had not yet applied were paired with trained mentors who taught them how to complete applications and essays, apply for financial aid, prepare for standardized tests, and successfully interview. Evaluators compared this supported evidence-based approach to a lighter touch intervention, which provided students with all the same information but no mentor. Those who worked with mentors were nearly twice as likely to attend a four-year college.[7]

Despite their necessity, mentoring alliances need not be as intensive and enduring as experts have commonly assumed. Researchers have found that moderate and strong mentoring relationships are equally effective in reducing delinquency and misconduct, and in improving school bonding and academic outcomes, whereas weak relationships are significantly less effective, or even harmful.[8] The same holds true in psychotherapy, where researchers have found that nonspecific factors such as the relationship and clinician characteristics are meaningfully related to outcomes, but do not solely account for client change.[9] Taken together, these studies demonstrate that there may be a threshold after which stronger relationships provide no additional benefits. In many cases, moderately close relationships may be good enough, particularly when they are balanced with evidence-based interventions.

A recent national study of school-based mentoring lends further support for striking a balance between relationship-building and targeted goals. The largest effects emerged in relationships that found the "sweet spot" between closeness and goal setting.[10] Moreover, the impact of structured, skills-based activities was stronger in the context of close relationships than in more distant relationships. These findings are consistent with those from a 2012 study of school-based mentoring matches, which found that taking a "sage/counseling" approach, in which mentors "balanced amicable engagement with adult guidance," resulted in better relationship quality (rated by both mentors and mentees) and greater declines in depression and aggression, compared to exclusively instrumental ("teaching assistant/tutoring") or relational ("friend/engaging") mentoring approaches.[11] Together, these studies suggest that mentoring programs should strive for a balance between building relationships and targeting specific goals and skills.

Of course, establishing a good working alliance (the first half of the above equation) is complicated by the fact that many children and adolescents are referred to mentoring programs by parents or teachers and, in some cases, may not even acknowledge that they need any additional support.[12] When young people feel that their participation is involuntary, they may resist mentors as adult authority figures telling them what to do. This sort of resistance, in turn, is an important signal to mentors to back off, slow down, and focus on building the alliance and positive expectations.[13] Resistance may also be a signal to get assistance from the mentoring program, particularly since weak, conflictual, or disappointing alliances can have damaging effects on youth.[14] Regardless of the particular issue, early detection and resolution can mitigate negative consequences. Indeed, because a personal relationship is at the heart of mentoring interventions, a lack of connection and consistency can touch on a youth's vulnerabilities in ways that can undermine the person's very sense of self.

This sort of sensitivity is common during the adolescent years, when issues of acceptance and rejection are particularly salient.[15] More than one hundred years ago, sociologist Charles Horton Cooley wrote about "the looking-glass self," wherein others become social mirrors into which adolescents look to form opinions of themselves.[16] Youth then integrate these opinions into their sense of self-worth. Another prominent sociologist, George Herbert Mead, built on this theory, suggesting that adolescents try to imagine how they are perceived from the perspective of important others, soaking in this "reflected appraisal" of praise and criticism.[17] As adolescents gain greater autonomy from their parents, appraisals by other adults can take on increased importance in ways that are beneficial and motivating, particularly for marginalized youth. For example, one study found that mentors' positive appraisal of marginalized students' personal qualities and performance was associated with higher self-esteem and greater well-being.[18] The reverse can also be true. In another study, adolescents paired with mentors who held generally more negative attitudes about youth showed fewer positive outcomes than those paired with more positively disposed mentors.[19] These studies highlight the importance of mentors' positive appraisals and attitudes when working with youth.

Showing this positive regard need not translate into "a stream of compliments."[20] It can sometimes be conveyed just as effectively through careful listening, speaking in a warm, gentle tone, and maintaining an interested and authentic stance.[21] In a recent study of cognitive behavioral therapy, perceived therapist genuineness was found to be the single most important predictor of the therapeutic alliance, and authenticity has been identified as an important component of mentoring.[22] Thus, a key step in establishing an alliance with youth is to convey a sense of being authentically engaged and invested.[23] This requires that mentors adopt a flexible, youth-centered, less formal style that is goal-oriented but also shaped by the mentee's interests, needs, and preferences.[24] Such stances enable mentors to strike the right balance between open-ended conversation, playful interactions, and relationship-building and the use of specific tools or curricula.

Being responsive in this way requires a fair amount of empathy, which is the capacity to be affected by and share someone else's emotional state and perspective.[25] Empathy can involve subtly matching posture and even the neural responses and feelings of another.[26] Also vital is "cultural empathy," which conveys respect for the values and perspectives of ethnic and racial minority groups.[27] This has implications for mentoring because volunteers and youth (and their families) may enter the relationship from markedly different classes and cultural worlds. Showing "cultural humility," as opposed to simply "competence," means being curious about and connecting with youth's most important and key identities (which could be their race/ethnicity, sexual orientation, generational status, nationality, etc.), and helping them to feel known and accepted.[28] As countries are shaped and transformed by global migration, such issues become even more salient. In the United States, for example, over one-quarter of the school-aged population are children of immigrants or immigrants themselves, representing nearly twenty million children under the age of eighteen.[29] Everyone has a cultural identity, not just nonmajority youth, and mentors who are respectful of and attuned to cultural beliefs and values will forge stronger alliances.[30] As recent research has highlighted, the same advice applies to working and interacting with mentees' parents and family members.

To understand effective adult-youth relationship processes, psychologist Marc Karver and his colleagues recently conducted a comprehensive meta-analysis of youth therapeutic alliances. His findings have direct relevance to building strong mentoring relationships. Across the twenty-eight studies, which encompassed 2,419 children and adolescents (with an average age of 12.38 years), there was a moderately strong association between the quality of the working alliance and youth outcomes (0.39), which is similar to findings reported in other meta-analyses.[31] Based on this comprehensive analysis, Karver and his colleagues made several research-driven suggestions for effective adult-youth relationship formation and maintenance (see Box 7.1).

Although focused on child and adolescent therapists, these suggestions apply to youth mentors, and include attitudes (e.g., being friendly, open, trusting, and culturally sensitive, and not taking mistrust personally) as well as recommendations for building strong alliances with parents and caregivers. Importantly, the researchers found that the therapist's relationship with caregivers was just as influential as the therapist-youth alliance in predicting youth outcomes. This underscores the importance of mentors and program staff building strong ties and mutual expectations, not only with their mentees, but with their mentees' caregivers and/or teachers. Even when mentors feel close to their mentees, when mentors fail to connect with parents, it can weaken their relationships with mentees, particularly when parents feel threatened by the bond.[32] Care-

Box 7.1: Building working alliances

Recommendations, based on a recent meta-analytic review of twenty-eight studies, for building strong adult-youth alliances. Excerpted with permission from Karver et al., "Meta-analysis of the Prospective Relation between Alliance and Outcome in Child and Adolescent Psychotherapy," *Psychotherapy* 55, no. 2 (2018): 341–355.

- **Create multiple alliances,** not only the alliance with the youth. The therapist–parent / caregiver association with treatment outcome is of the same magnitude as the therapist–youth alliance.

- **Avoid being overly formal,** emphasizing common ground that comes off as inauthentic, "pushing" youth to talk about or overly focusing on emotionally sensitive material, bringing up previous material to discuss before they are ready or too frequently, and criticizing youth clients; these are therapist behaviors that undermine the alliance.

- **Seek to manifest a friendly disposition** (even fun / humorous when appropriate), provide praise, show impartiality (not automatically taking the parental point of view), and demonstrate genuine respect for the youth clients while calmly and attentively eliciting information in an interactive manner about the youth's subjective experience; these are therapist behaviors that promote the alliance. Only gradually address deeper issues after starting on current practical concerns.

- **Do not take initial mistrust personally;** youths, especially adolescents, are not likely to come to therapy ready to trust a therapist who they often perceive to be another adult authority figure.

(continued)

Box 7.1 (continued)

- **Earn trust and form an alliance by establishing confidentiality,** carefully attending (using active / reflective listening methods) to the youth's perspective, showing empathy so that the client feels understood, accepting / validating and seeing value in youth statements, and advocating for the youth and presenting as an ally. Also critical is expressing support for the youth client especially when emotionally painful material is discussed.

- **Expect and honor divergent views** about treatment goals and how to accomplish them. Formation of a therapeutic alliance with both youth and parent(s) requires the therapist to be open to suggestions / ideas and to collaboratively formulate goals and treatment plans that are responsive to youths and parents.

- **Acknowledge parental strengths and collaborate,** partner, and set mutual expectations with a youth's caregivers in a relaxed manner. If parents are not adequately engaged in treatment, they will not bring a youth client even if the youth does enjoy a good relationship with the therapist.

- **Socialize the youth to treatment** by providing an explicit, consistent, and credible framework for how the planned treatment is supposed to work, orienting the youth to the therapist and client roles in treatment, and establishing hopefulness / expectancy that the treatment will be useful in the client's life.

- **Create a psychotherapy environment in which the youth client feels like a partner** in the relationship and maintain flexibility to respond to youth needs even when delivering a manualized treatment. Youth, especially adolescents, are unlikely to remain engaged in treatment if they perceive the therapist to be another adult authority figure who tells them what to do.

- **Match or adapt alliance-enhancing behaviors** and overall approach to a youth client based on his or her developmental level, gender, cultural background, attributional style, readiness to change, treatment preferences, interpersonal skills, and attachment style.

- **Make adjustments in alliance formation** based on parental characteristics (interpersonal skills, level of stress, expectancies on degree of parental involvement in treatment, and cultural values) and on any match / mismatch between parent–youth perspectives.

givers should be provided with ample opportunity to voice their hopes and concerns and to provide details and specify priorities for the relationship. It is often caregivers who initiate the mentoring, and they are typically most familiar with any other issues that affect their children's well-being. Given the importance of caregiver perspectives, John Weisz and colleagues have developed and validated a strategy in which youth and their caregivers separately list, rank, and describe the problems that concern them most. The top three problems identified by each are then used to help determine treatment and are regularly assessed.[33] This approach can inform program staff and focus intervention and assessment efforts on those issues that youth and caregivers consider most important.

Unfortunately, when programs do take parents into account, it is sometimes to manage what is perceived as their potentially intrusive, obstructive, or otherwise negative influence on the development of the mentoring relationship.[34] These approaches to parents and other caregivers may stem from the perception of mentoring as compensating for an inadequate family life. Indeed, recent research on mentors' perceptions in a large, multisite program revealed that, although mentors focused on their mentees' strengths, they viewed mentees' parents and communities primarily as negative influences.[35]

Other researchers have also highlighted the importance of communication and agreement among parents and other stakeholders, noting that there are actually four key people (the mentee, the mentor, the mentoring program staff member, and the parent) that need to be considered, since any one of them can make or break the bond.[36] Thus, in addition to supporting youth and caregivers, effective programs provide adequate training, supervision, and support to mentors. A recent study of over 3,200 matches showed that the two strongest predictors of match retention were ongoing mentor supervision and staff-to-mentor ratios.[37] Staff with lighter caseloads can provide training that helps support more effective, enduring, and higher-quality mentoring relationships. Such training, in turn, affects the quality of mentor-mentee relationships; prematch mentor training has been shown to predict mentors' relationship satisfaction and commitment.[38] In a meta-analysis of fifty-five program evaluations, researchers found higher effect sizes for those programs that followed "best practices" including screening of volunteers, careful matching, providing parent support, and having clear expectations and communication around the frequency of meetings and length of the match.[39] Programs that followed six or more effective mentoring practices showed effect sizes that were five times larger than programs that followed fewer than six of these practices (0.20 vs. 0.04). Clearly, programs can tip the balance toward success by following evidence-based practices.

Fortunately, there are a growing number of resources to help both youth mentoring programs and mentors succeed. MENTOR's National Mentoring Resource Center provides excellent training and research summaries for programs and the *Chronicle of Evidence-Based Mentoring* offers a searchable database of research and evaluation summaries. Likewise, MENTOR's Elements of Effective Practice (EEPM) outlines standards that programs can adopt to advance relationship quality. Many mentoring practitioners are already familiar with the EEPM, which first emerged in 1990 as a somewhat unwieldy grab bag of ideas but has since evolved into a clear set of safety and evidence-informed standards. Now in its fourth edition, the EEPM describes best practices for mentor recruitment, screening, training, matching, monitoring, and support, as well as strategies for ending relationships. Adherence to the EEPM, especially the training standards, has been shown to lead to longer matches.[40] Yet, a recent analysis of data from forty-five mentoring programs representing nearly thirty thousand relationships showed that about one-third of programs provided their mentors with less than the recommended minimum two hours of prematch training, and only 13 percent of programs contacted each mentor and mentee at the recommended minimum frequency of twice in the first month and then once monthly thereafter.[41] This represents lost opportunities for catching early problems with mentors and ensuring successful matches.

These relationship-building standards cut across all program models. When blended with targeted treatment and scaled through prevention science practices, they can help to address the most pressing issues facing today's youth. In fact, as described in Chapter 8, embracing treatment and prevention science will put the field of youth mentoring on the road to rigor.

8

The Road to Rigor

Youth mentoring programs sit at the nexus of treatment and prevention science, offering both the structure for forging helping relationships and the apparatus for scaling them. Thus, they are exceptionally well-positioned to benefit from the lessons and innovations from both fields. Treatment science provides the rationale and resources for developing theoretically informed, practically applicable helping approaches that serve youth more effectively. As I discussed in earlier chapters, the burgeoning field of mental health apps (MHapps) and other technology-delivered interventions has the potential to provide large, nonspecific programs with access to a growing array of targeted, evidence-based interventions. Prevention science provides a framework for the implementation, evaluation, and dissemination of effective programs across different settings, youth, cultures, and ethnicities. And, to the extent that programs begin to think of volunteers as paraprofessional helpers and begin to harness all that is relevant from treatment and prevention science, they will be better positioned to deliver effective care.

Psychologist John Weisz and his colleagues have provided a roadmap to materialize this vision—one that the field of mentoring would be wise to follow—that involves:

Identifying effective programs that address the most common problems and disorders facing young people, paying careful attention to their effective adoption across different ethnicities and cultures, . . . specifying the conditions under which programs are most effective and, importantly, the "change mechanisms" that underlie these positive effects and . . . testing interventions across various contexts, and, once proven, disseminating them in ways that make them accessible and effective across a broad range of community and practice settings.[1]

Building on these recommendations, as well as recent research across both treatment and prevention science, the field would benefit from the following strategies:

Prioritize mental health and well-being: Although youth mentoring programs should continue to target the full range of issues (such as academic performance, civic engagement, college access, and job skills), mental health and wellness are particularly promising priorities. The basic contours of formal mentoring relationships follow those of professional helping relationships (e.g., often meeting once a week in mostly one-on-one relationships), and many youth mentees present with acute symptoms of anxiety; depression; and social, emotional, and behavioral struggles that impede their academic performance and other long-term goals. Mental health concerns are often what prompt parent and teacher referrals, and mentoring programs are particularly successful in moving the needle on depression in vulnerable youth.[2]

Shift professional mental health tasks to mentors: Particularly in light of the global shortage of mental health providers and other youth-serving professionals, the length and cost of professional training, the expense and difficulties associated with accessing mental health and wellness services, and the stigma and distrust that professional services carry in many marginalized communities, mentors should be trained and supervised to support and/or deliver evidence-based care, and to more effectively "give psychology away." As we move in this direction, programs should find ways to directly recognize and credential the work of their volunteers.

Calibrate risk to intervention approach: Programs should determine mentees' most salient challenges, identify the best, evidence-based approach to employ, and then match them to mentors with the experience necessary to effectively support them. Children who do not have immediate, identifiable challenges may be better served by recreational programs where they can interact informally with multiple adults. Given the limited pool of volunteers, only about 5 percent of US children and adolescents can be served by mentoring programs and not every child needs or wants the level of structure that they provide.[3] Formal mentoring relationships should thus be viewed as an early, nonstigmatizing source of paraprofessional support that is less intensive than professional counseling but more structured than natural mentoring support. Just as youth are not referred to therapists or other specialists simply for companionship, the same should hold true in formal mentoring programs.

Shift mentors' roles from delivering to supporting interventions: In contrast to specialized mentoring programs, which can target particular issues and populations, large, nonspecific programs like Big Brothers Big Sisters cannot be expected to deliver the full range of targeted, evidence-based services required to effectively address their mentees' diverse needs. Rather than deliver interventions, mentors in nonspecific programs should be trained to support their mentees' engagement in targeted, evidence-based interventions delivered by professionals (embedded mentoring) or through technology (blended mentoring).

Of course, lurking behind any recommendation for improving mentoring programs are the upstream problems of poverty and growing inequality, and all that they entail for families—housing instability, schools with inadequate resources, limited health care, and unsafe neighborhoods. The list goes on. Program staff members are well aware of this oppressive backdrop and the reality that time spent with a mentor could never be enough to redress these concerns. The same holds true in child and adolescent therapy, which psychologist Payton Jones and his colleagues recently acknowledged is in

> a kind of competition with all that happens during the other 110+ waking hours, and many of the forces that can contribute to psychological distress and dysfunction during those hours may not be readily altered by therapy. From this perspective, it may make sense to construe youth psychotherapy as but one of many forces that can impact youth mental health and functioning, and in many cases not the most powerful of those forces.[4]

Not only are mentoring relationships one of many competing forces in the lives of youth, some argue that volunteering through nonprofit programs (particularly those supported by corporate philanthropy) may actually divert our attention from larger solutions. From this perspective, limited charitable efforts are essentially feel-good solutions to larger social problems, serving as a moral safety valve that relieves the pressure on citizens, governments, and corporations to grapple in more meaningful ways with the root causes of poverty and inequality.[5] And, by narrowly targeting skills, such as those for managing stress and anxiety, programs are essentially asking children to muster solutions to counter these challenges. Taking stock of such issues in youth mentoring, in 2007 Gary Walker, then president of Public/Private Ventures, wrote:

> At its core, mentoring is a charitable act, a kindness to a stranger, improvement in the life of people one at a time—whereas what we need is social change, where change comes to larger groups of individuals all at once. Mentoring as social policy, under this critique, is diversionary at best, reactionary at worst. Even if it is effective and does build confidence in social policy, it remains diversionary and/or reactionary because what it builds is confidence in the capacity of individuals to help individuals; it blunts the fundamental need for broader social change.[6]

As Walker points out, however, helping a young person while also doing whatever we can to address the broader context of inequality and stress is not a zero-sum game. In fact, when equipped with targeted, evidence-based interventions, a well-trained volunteer mentor is one of our best hopes for providing mental health and other services to the young people who need them most, resolving early problems and preventing negative cascades into more serious difficulties. Short-term expenditures in early, targeted intervention programs are offset by reductions in more costly downstream social, health, and correctional services.[7] Likewise, early skills training positions children to benefit from later education and interventions. For example, mentors can teach youth social and emotional regulation skills that can act as a sort of immune system, enabling them to marshal defenses as stressors arise. In other instances, conversations between mentors and mentees can heighten youth's critical thinking about broader societal issues, providing "an opportunity for marginalized youth to reclaim power, celebrate their identities, and take ownership of their narratives."[8] More generally, by creating meaningful connections between volunteers and marginalized youth, and providing opportunities for volunteers to gain a deeper understanding of the everyday challenges such youth face, the field of mentoring can help to bridge perspectives. In our increasingly segregated world, mentoring programs provide a sanctioned channel for unlikely connections across widely diverse ethnic, cultural, and economic lines.

Speaking to the Wesleyan University 2016 graduating class, the director of the Equal Justice Initiative, Bryan A. Stevenson, highlighted the benefits of such connections, and the importance of

> getting proximate to the places in our nation, in our world, where there's suffering and abuse and neglect. Many of you have been taught your whole lives that there are parts of the community where the schools don't work very well; if there are sections of the community where there's a lot of violence or abuse or despair or neglect, you should stay as far away from those parts of town as possible. Today, I want to urge you to do the opposite. I think you need to get closer to the parts of the communities where you live where there's suffering and abuse and neglect. I want you to choose to get closer. We have people trying to solve problems from a distance, and their solutions don't work, because until you get close, you don't understand the nuances and the details of those problems.[9]

From a distance, it is easier to dehumanize and blame young people for their struggles. Mentoring can help counter that tendency. In the words of anthropologist Margaret Mead, "It is extraordinarily difficult to love children in the abstract, to devote oneself exclusively to the next generation. It is only through precise, attentive knowledge of particular children that we become—as we must—informed advocates for the needs of all children."[10]

As long as mentors can generalize their concern for their one mentee to a concern for children in similar situations, programs have an important role in both bridging gaps in mental health services and catalyzing authentic action and reform. Even so, there will remain a large gap between the number of youth who could benefit from targeted, evidence-based mentoring and those who have access to it. Many programs have long waitlists and struggle to recruit and retain a sufficient number of volunteers. Given this scarcity, there is wisdom to reserving volunteer mentors for those youth who could benefit from structured approaches. Other youth, such as those in need of more general friendship, recreational opportunities, and support, could be provided with the training and encouragement to identify and recruit caring, prosocial adults from within their extended families, schools, after-school programs, and communities. This will require a more intentional mobilization and recruitment of the many people who are already living, working, worshipping, and retiring in youth's communities.

9

WHY WE CAN'T LEAVE NATURAL MENTORING TO CHANCE

In Chapters 5 and 6, I outlined several mentoring approaches (specialized, embedded, and blended) that can help to align mentoring with the broader fields of prevention and treatment. Yet, even if we get all this right, the stubborn fact remains that only a small fraction of children and adolescents are served by mentoring programs. As with mental health providers, there are simply not enough trained mentors to go around—and not every child needs or wants this level of structure. Some youth may need more adult support, guidance, and friendship, as opposed to the more deliberate goal-focused approaches described above. The good news is that over 70 percent of surveyed youth report having a natural mentor.[1] The key will be to develop interventions and incentives that support and democratize this valuable resource. In this chapter, I describe *youth-initiated mentoring* (YIM) approaches, which train youth to value, identify, and recruit natural mentors. This hybrid model brings together the strengths of informal mentoring relationships with the infrastructure and support provided by formal mentoring programs, while empowering adolescents to identify, draw upon, and strengthen existing support.

In his book *Our Kids: The American Dream in Crisis,* sociologist Robert Putnam highlights the fact that, of the roughly two-thirds of youth in the United States who reported having had a mentor, fewer than 5 percent derived their mentoring solely from formal mentoring programs. Instead, the vast majority of mentoring takes place outside the realm of mentoring programs (e.g., in families, neighborhoods, and schools). Putnam's analysis also revealed that informal mentoring lasted about thirty months on average, which is far longer than formal relationships. Thus, combining frequency and duration, he estimated youth in the United States receive about eight times as much informal as formal mentoring.[2]

On the face of it, these data could be taken to suggest that there are already plenty of caring adults out there and that the majority of young people are perfectly adept at enlisting them to help support their developmental needs. Yet, by uncomfortable margins, affluent youth are far more likely than youth in the lowest income quartile to have natural mentors. Indeed, with the exception of extended family members, youth in the top socioeconomic status quartile report dramatically more natural mentoring across every category of adult (e.g., teachers, coaches, and employers).[3] More recently, large-scale studies have shown that natural mentoring relationships are more helpful, but far less available, to economically disadvantaged youth relative to their more privileged counterparts. Many of these studies stem from the ongoing, five-wave National Longitudinal Study of Adolescent to Adult Health (Add Health), a treasure trove of data collected from over twenty thousand American students across more than one hundred middle schools and high schools from 1979 to the present.[4] Although it is impossible to determine the causal influence of natural mentor relationships (they cannot randomly be assigned), new statistical techniques have helped to control for some of the selection biases inherent in studying their effects.[5] Drawing from the Add Health data set, researchers have shown that adolescents and young adults who are able to identify at least one supportive nonparent mentor in their lives tend to engage in less risk-taking behavior; have improved psychological and social functioning; achieve higher educational attainment, higher salaries, and more intrinsically rewarding jobs; and have better career outcomes.[6] Other data sets have shown similar associations. For example, a recent Gallup-Purdue Index survey of sixty thousand college graduates found associations between having mentors in college and graduation, work engagement, and overall well-being. As the lead author notes:

> We learned that if graduates felt supported during college—by professors who cared, made them excited about learning and who encouraged them to pursue their goals and dreams—their odds of being engaged in work more than doubled, as did their odds of thriving in their well-being. This finding was true of graduates of all ages and years of graduation; in other words, it's a career- and life-trajectory game changer.[7]

In a report following up the Gallup-Purdue Index findings, researchers found that students who had college mentors reported greater life satisfaction later on in life. Other researchers have emphasized the connection between natural mentors and academic success, school connectedness, perceptions of the importance of education, and later civic engagement.[8] Finally, my colleagues and I recently conducted the first comprehensive meta-analysis of natural mentoring, encompassing thirty studies that, since 1992, have measured the effects of natural mentoring on a range of youth outcomes including social, academic, and vocational functioning.[9] The presence of any natural mentor led to a modest improvement (0.24), and a moderate positive effect (0.42) resulted when the quality of the natural mentoring relationship (i.e., frequency of contact, support, and relationship duration) was taken into account. Additionally, consistent with the research on formal mentoring, larger effects were found for mentors with a helping profession background (e.g., teachers, guidance counselors, religious leaders, and doctors/therapists).[10] Particularly for youth who do not have access to such adults through their families and communities, these relationships proved to be vitally important.

Unfortunately, as are so many other valuable resources, well-connected natural mentors are unequally distributed—and those neighborhoods and schools that are already rich in natural mentors are only getting richer.[11] The social fabric is stretched particularly thin in low-income urban communities. Manufacturing jobs that once provided families and neighborhoods with some measure of economic stability have given way to low-paying service jobs that make it difficult for poor families to form bridges to the middle class. Many communities, particularly those with high concentrations of black families, have been depleted of higher-income adults, who once served as respected authority figures. Many such adults have moved out of urban centers, causing gradual depopulation and, along with it, income segregation. Although the gaps in earning disparities between other racial and cultural groups have narrowed over time, black-white disparities have persisted across generations. These disparities can be explained, in part, by unemployment and deteriorating conditions in many predominantly black urban neighborhoods.[12] Reflecting on these trends, sociologist William Julius Wilson noted that it is nearly impossible to reproduce in white communities the structural circumstances under which many black Americans live, including the historical legacy of extended racial discrimination and segregation across the generations. . . . Very few urban white neighborhoods, even those with the same poverty rates as black neighborhoods, approximate these conditions.[13]

Neighborhood disadvantages are then amplified in nearby schools, where budget constraints translate into fewer teachers, guidance counselors, nurses, and mental health providers per student, and fewer opportunities for the sorts of school-sponsored athletics and extracurricular activities that give rise to informal connections with coaches and other caring adults.[14] School professionals are sometimes the only college-educated adults that marginalized youth routinely encounter, making them vitally important for connecting youth to new opportunities.

Although marginalized students often feel closer to the natural mentors in their extended family and friendship circles, school staff and teacher-mentors are better able to provide support and information that can help the students advance in school and jobs.[15] A growing body of literature has highlighted the vital role of teachers and school staff as mentors to marginalized students.[16] A close relationship with a teacher can boost students' academic motivation, interest, and performance, as well as their overall attachment to school, over and above parent and family support.[17] In fact, some experts have concluded that at least one strong relationship with a teacher is the "single most important ingredient" for vulnerable adolescents' academic development and success.[18] Others have highlighted the lifelong educational and economic benefits of being assigned to even one good teacher.[19] High school and college students who list a teacher or guidance counselor as their mentor have better academic and job outcomes than youth with mentors from outside of school (e.g., extended family, religious leaders, or neighbors).[20] Such adults enable students to connect to new opportunities and networks, and to more fully engage in school.[21]

Analyses of the Add Health study have indicated that teachers are the single most commonly nominated type of mentors (10 percent), a rate that is more than double maternal grandmothers (4.8 percent), uncles (4.6 percent), religious leaders (4.1 percent), and employers (4.2 percent).[22] Even after controlling for academic achievement, having a teacher-mentor was associated with a greater likelihood of high school graduation, enrollment in post-high school education and vocational training, and completion of a four-year college degree.[23] But here's the rub. Students who nominate teacher-mentors are both more affluent and attend better schools.[24] More generally, students from lower socioeconomic backgrounds are far less likely to report having high-quality ties and mentorships with teachers and guidance counselors and, in fact, report lower overall relationship quality with these important adults.[25] In addition to the relative scarcity of teacher-mentors, less advantaged youth do not feel the same sense of entitlement to their teachers' support, and are less likely than their upper- and middle-class peers to seek help from them.[26] Less-advantaged youth have not been socialized to think strategically about cultivating and maintaining these ties and are less likely to have help from their parents in managing their relationships with teachers, with whom strong connections can have lasting positive effects.[27]

In addition to in-school mentoring resources, marginalized youth have far less access to after-school programs, summer camps, competitive sports teams, youth arts, and other programs that can lead to strong natural mentor ties.[28] The adults staffing such programs are often relatively young themselves, and oftentimes from the same communities that they serve, making them more familiar with the underlying culture. They are thus are well-positioned to connect with adolescents and offer them credible role modeling, advice, and guidance.[29] Moreover, they have fewer curricular demands than teachers and more opportunities to engage in informal conversations and enjoyable activities with students that foster close bonds. Psychologist Bart Hirsch and colleagues analyzed low-income youth's relationships with staff in several Boys and Girls Clubs across Chicago. Club staff were found to offer a distinct form of support, falling somewhere between the caring and love received from extended family and the specific targeted skills received from teachers. Most youth attended the clubs every day and three-quarters of the adolescents considered it a second home. Unfortunately, school- and community-based after-school programs, particularly those for low-income youth, tend to have fewer resources and annual staff turnover rates as high as 40 percent.[30] This represents lost opportunities for natural mentoring.

Other studies have explored the vital role that athletic programs and coaches can play, including student exposure to coaches who not only help advance athletic skills, but also promote self-confidence and self-discipline.[31] Drawing on the Add Health data, my colleagues and I found that students who nominated an athletic coach as their mentor were more likely to complete high school and college, *even after* accounting for the influence of participation in sports and academic functioning. And—you guessed it—students from poorer backgrounds and those attending poorer schools were significantly less likely than their more privileged peers to nominate a coach mentor.[32] Thus, although they stand to gain the most from a mentoring relationship, youth from lower socioeconomic groups are often the least likely to report having a natural mentor. Moreover, the natural mentoring relationships forged by youth from low-income backgrounds appear to be less likely to provide connections to new opportunities than those of more privileged youth.

To understand this difference, it helps to know a little about social capital. Researchers have theorized about different types of social networks, and the need for a balance between so-called "strong" and "weak" ties.[33] For youth, strong ties involve relationships with close family and friends who are relatively similar in terms of race and social class, while weak ties involve a broader network of relationships with nonfamilial others, such as teachers, guidance counselors, coaches, and employers who can serve as a bridge to new connections, knowledge, and expertise that facilitates upward mobility. In disadvantaged families, strong ties, while crucial sources of support, are typically less able to connect youth to educational and occupational opportunities and tend to be more focused on ensuring the child's safety and regulating problem behavior.[34] By contrast, adults outside close-knit circles may have more authority and power, enabling them to serve as "institutional agents" who can provide marginalized youth with the cultural and social capital necessary to navigate unfamiliar settings and opportunities.[35]

In a recent study, my colleagues and I drew on the Add Health data to explore how economic disadvantage constrains the availability and nature of natural mentoring relationships. Adolescents whose families received public assistance and/or lived in poor neighborhoods had less access to natural mentors. They forged more bonds with family and friend adults (i.e., strong ties) than with teachers or employers (i.e., weak ties). Moreover, their relationships

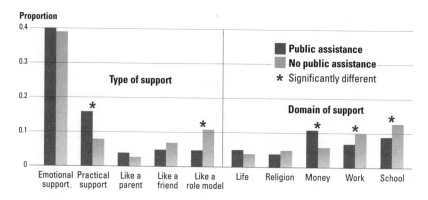

FIGURE 9.1: TYPES AND DOMAINS OF NATURAL MENTOR SUPPORT BY PUBLIC ASSISTANCE RECEIPT: Youth whose families are on public assistance receive less future-oriented support and are less likely than more privileged youth to view their mentors as role models. Asterisks indicate statistically significant differences ($p < 0.05$).

were more likely to focus on practical support around issues such as finances and less likely to be sources of role modeling and future-oriented school, identity, or work advice (see Figure 9.1). These findings suggest that natural mentoring varies across social class in ways that reproduce inequality.

More recently, my colleague and I found that having a school or other institutionally connected mentor was associated with higher educational attainment and higher household incomes *twenty years later,* while family and neighborhood mentors conferred none of these benefits.[36] And, although teachers and more socially connected mentors are less available to marginalized youth, such youth are far more likely to benefit from them.[37] This is because the dense and privileged social networks of youth from wealthier families can often compensate for any lost opportunities to deeply connect with caring adults at school. But when students come from less-affluent families, the effects of teacher support on academic outcomes are stronger.[38] Drawing on a large national sample of high school graduates, researchers recently showed that having a natural mentor promoted college attendance among poor and working-class youth, but did not affect this outcome in middle- and upper-class youth.[39] Similarly, drawing from the Add Health data set, researchers have found that positive associations between school-based natural mentors and later educational attainment were strongest among youth from more marginalized socioeconomic and racial backgrounds.[40] Particularly since only 9 percent of students in the bottom income quartile earn a bachelor's degree by age twenty-four (compared to 77 percent from the top quartile), mentors have a particularly important role to play in marginalized students' success.

Even when more marginalized youth do find mentors and somehow make it to college, educational and employment systems have a way of magnifying disparities, stacking the odds in favor of more privileged but similarly credentialed students. Psychologist Katherine Milkman and her colleagues have demonstrated how implicit biases on the part of teachers can affect access to learning experiences, mentorship, and employment. She and her team sent emails to over 6,500 professors across 89 disciplines and 259 institutions. The professors believed the emails were from students expressing interest in graduate study and research opportunities. Email requests were identical except for students' names, which were carefully selected to indicate ethnicity and gender. Across all academic fields, except for fine arts, professors were significantly more responsive to emails from students with names suggesting that they were white males than they were to emails from students with names suggesting that they were women or minority students.[41]

These biases then follow students into the job market, where employers are more likely to respond to resumes that signify privilege. Sociologists Lauren Rivera and András Tilcsik sent resumes to potential employers at law firms. The employers believed that the resumes were from students expressing interest in summer internships. The resumes listed similar credentials, but by tweaking the extracurricular activities and interests, they were able to signify social class (e.g., sailing team, polo, and classical music vs. track and field, pick-up soccer, and country music). Applicants with higher-class signifiers received significantly more callbacks for job interviews. As the authors conclude, "despite our national myth that anyone can make it if they work hard enough, the social class people grow up in greatly shapes the types of jobs (and salaries) they can attain, regardless of the achievements listed on their resumes."[42] Better jobs and salaries, along with the social networks that result from them, continue the cycles of inequality and underemployment for less privileged young adults. In a study that used machine learning to aggregate educational and employment data from millions of resumes, researchers showed that students who found jobs that matched their level of education (i.e., they were "appropriately employed") right out of school continued to do so in the decades that followed, while those who started out underemployed got caught in a cycle of underemployment that became progressively difficult to escape.[43] The families that consolidate their privilege, connections, and access to good jobs may be unaware of the extent to which the system is rigged in their favor. Educational opportunities, legacy admissions, and nepotism accrue so quietly over a wealthy young person's lifespan that they are often folded into one's sense of entitlement.

Several years ago, I had the opportunity to attend a Princeton University commencement address by writer Michael Lewis, who described a study in which experimenters divided a sample of college students into teams of three.[44] The teams were then tasked with solving a moral problem or social issue, with one person per team randomly assigned to be its leader. After thirty minutes, the experimenters interrupted the teams to provide them with a plate of four cookies. Each participant took one cookie, leaving just one left over for someone to take. Participants who were randomly ascribed the "leader" role were more likely to grab that second cookie. As Lewis describes:

> With incredible consistency the person arbitrarily appointed
> leader of the group grabbed the fourth cookie and ate it. Not only
> ate it, but ate it with gusto: lips smacking, mouth open, drool at
> the corners of their mouths. In the end all that was left of the
> extra cookie was crumbs on the leader's shirt. This leader had
> performed no special task. He had no special virtue. He'd been
> chosen at random, 30 minutes earlier. His status was nothing but
> luck. But it still left him with the sense that the cookie should
> be his.[45]

Lewis then turned to the Princeton graduates:

> In a general sort of way you have been appointed the leader of
> the group. Your appointment may not be entirely arbitrary. But
> you must sense its arbitrary aspect: you are the lucky few. Lucky
> in your parents, lucky in your country, lucky that a place like
> Princeton exists that can take in lucky people, introduce them to
> other lucky people, and increase their chances of becoming even
> luckier. Lucky that you live in the richest society the world has
> ever seen, in a time when no one actually expects you to sacrifice
> your interests to anything. All of you have been faced with the

extra cookie. All of you will be faced with many more of them. In time you will find it easy to assume that you deserve the extra cookie. For all I know, you may. But you'll be happier, and the world will be better off, if you at least pretend that you don't.[46]

It is only on such rare occasions that the winners of life's lottery are asked to reflect on the depth and luck of their unearned privilege. For more advantaged youth, it is easy to forget how much luck is involved in finding a natural mentor who can open doors to amazing opportunities—from access to mentor-rich and privilege-signifying schools and extracurricular activities to having well-connected parents, friends, and neighbors. Although in isolation each opportunity may seem inconsequential, their cumulative impact strengthens a system that further disadvantages already marginalized youth. As income inequality and class-based segregation increases, it sharply limits social mobility. Natural mentors may seem like great equalizers, but their distribution naturally bends toward perpetuating, rather than redressing, inequality.

Youth-Initiated Mentoring Models

Fortunately, a growing number of innovative programs have emerged that successfully target the social fragmentation and isolation that affect so many communities. The approaches involve both teaching youth to "fish" for mentors (i.e., to recruit natural mentors) and "stocking the pond" (i.e., expanding the availability of high-social capital adults in marginalized youth's lives). The National Guard Youth Challenge Program, an intensive quasimilitary program for adolescents who have dropped out of high school, has successfully deployed the youth-initiated mentoring approach.[47] In

Connected Scholars, an extension of this approach, high school and college students are provided with the strategies and skills to cultivate a network of supportive adults, rather than a single mentoring relationship. Compared to incoming college students who were provided only with information, incoming students who were assigned to a four-session intervention in which they learned how to recruit faculty and staff support had stronger ties with faculty members, higher grade-point averages, and less help avoidance at the end of their freshman year.[48] Other networking approaches help students choose a nonparental adult to attend skill-building workshops with them or help to connect youth who are aging out of (or at risk of entering) the foster care system.[49] Most recently, researchers have shown that suicidal youth who learned to recruit caring adults had lower levels of mortality nearly fifteen years later than their counterparts who did not.[50]

Of course, the onus for locating and recruiting mentors need not rest solely with youth. Adults in many settings—such as schools, Little League, juvenile courts, neighborhoods, and workplaces—are afforded many opportunities to mentor youth. But, because mentoring is typically seen as a byproduct but not a central mission of many youth services and settings, adults are rarely provided with specific training around building strong relationships. A range of factors, from frequent staff turnover to fears of being accused of acting inappropriately, can further dampen adults' willingness to build strong intergenerational relationships.[51] Thus, in addition to teaching youth to fish, strategies that effectively "stock the pond" with trained, intentionally supportive adults will be vitally important in the years ahead.

Although retired adults could help "stock the ponds" of schools and other settings, they are provided with remarkably few opportunities and little encouragement to interact with unrelated young people. Nearly a third of adults over fifty-five live in communities that comprise mostly or entirely people their age, and more than 90 percent of people over sixty report that they never discuss "important matters" with nonfamily members under thirty-six.[52] Yet, with adults over fifty outnumbering youth under eighteen for the first time in American history, this age segregation represents lost opportunities for mutually beneficial natural mentoring relationships.[53]

In this chapter, I have argued for a more inclusive model of mentoring—one that expands the focus from formal one-on-one "treatment" approaches to more broadly strengthening networks of supportive intergenerational connections. When finding a natural mentor is left to chance, the odds favor more privileged youth. Such youth grow up in settings with greater access to the kinds of caring adults who can serve as role models that connect them to further educational and career networks and opportunities. Addressing this inequality will require that we ensure that disadvantaged settings develop innovative ways to support youth's capacity to find and recruit such adults. The field of youth mentoring is ripe for this sort of innovation.

10

The Future of Mentoring

The findings presented in this book are both a wake-up call and a call to action. Decades of mentoring program investment and research have failed to move the needle on youth outcomes and, despite being generally less effective than targeted evidence-based approaches, nonspecific "friendship" models remain dominant. Many mentoring program staff and volunteers feel overwhelmed and ill-equipped to work with the increasingly vulnerable youth that programs are being asked to serve. These struggles are persisting against a background of record inequality, imbalanced opportunities, climbing rates of youth distress, a fiercely competitive funding landscape, and a consensus in the broader helping fields that decisions should be informed by the best available research and economic evidence.[1]

Nonetheless, conceptual ambiguities and cognitive biases in our field, often evoked by the vocabulary of mentoring, have enabled us to bypass conventional norms of scientific rigor and program implementation. Instead, the field continues to exercise unusual license to improvise and avoid the consequences of disappointing findings. Such tendencies have been further fueled by a cacophony of misleading claims and wide discrepancies between researchers and practitioners in beliefs about what constitutes scientific evidence.

Fortunately, advances in clinical and prevention science provide a roadmap for improving youth outcomes. The mentoring programs that will thrive in the future will be those that demonstrate a clear return on investment over the relatively short term and can be delivered in ways that ensure standardization and easy, straightforward use. These criteria have led to improved effectiveness and cost-effectiveness across the fields of both medicine and mental health care alike; the same will be true for mentoring.[2]

Much remains to be done to understand the complexities and effectiveness of the new approaches to mentoring presented in this book, and to determine the settings and circumstances in which both formal and natural mentoring can make their biggest impact. Many of the suggested approaches to mentoring interventions are in the early stages of development and currently lack the track record and the accumulated program wisdom of traditional mentoring programs. New programs that deliver specialized mentoring interventions, as well as new models that shift volunteer roles from delivering to supporting interventions, will need to be evaluated. Research that directly compares nonspecific, friendship approaches to specialized, blended, embedded, and youth-initiated approaches to mentoring is needed. Such studies will lead to a deeper understanding of the active ingredients and the right balance of common factors and specific approaches. The structured goals and tools, whatever their specific value, may actually contribute to relationship rituals that inspire hope and fuel self-efficacy.[3] Nevertheless, it will be essential to explore whether the adoption of these more targeted, goal-oriented approaches can peacefully coexist with the essential task of relationship formation. To this end, volunteers will need the training and support to strike a balance between friendship and goals, and guard against rigidity and the impulse to put goal attainment above relationship formation and maintenance. This will involve finesse, flexibility, and a willingness to suspend or abandon planned lessons and activities when adherence contributes to an erosion of relationship-building and trust. Striking this balance will improve mentor retention and ensure that the field retains its central identity and mission of providing relationship-based change.[4]

Moreover, as mentors take on more paraprofessional roles and partner with more advanced supervisors, programs should find ways to more explicitly recognize and credential volunteer service. Just as the field has been slow to dispense with idealized notions of mentoring bonds and either-or thinking about relationships and skills, the implicit, falsely dichotomous belief that volunteers hold only altruistic motivations, and that career, academic, or other "egoistic" motivations somehow taint their service, has impeded programs' capacity to facilitate mentors' professional goals. Although such goals are thought to undermine volunteer retention and effectiveness, the scientific literature has not supported this supposition.[5] As any teacher or therapist knows, deriving educational or professional benefits from service does not diminish the sense of pride and joy that comes with feeling genuinely helpful to someone. To the extent that programs recognize the inherently transactional nature of volunteer mentoring, they can more directly reap the full benefits of a truly engaged volunteer workforce.

There will be other challenges as mentoring programs take on new service modes. First, stepped-care models will require mentor and program staff access to more highly trained, professional supervisors. Similarly, more specialized care may entail costs such as licensing fees for validated assessment tools, evidence-based curricula, and mental health applications. Although programs often balk at such expenditures and opt instead to rely on homegrown tools and trainings, it will be important to consider the opportunity costs, and the better return on investment, of more effective models. Corporate contributions to support additional staff and tools can help to offset the negative effects of record inequality which are, once again, putting a "tax upon the future" of a generation of marginalized youth. Additionally, embedding mentors in schools, mental health settings, and other contexts is likely to require additional coordination. Ultimately, however, these shifts toward supporting roles will enable nonspecialized mentoring programs to focus their resources on what they do best—recruit, screen, train, and supervise volunteers to form productive alliances.

Even with additional recruitment and retention efforts, and more limited, defined, and effective mentor involvement, there will never be enough volunteer mentors to go around. As such, the limited pool of volunteers should be reserved for those who need this more focused, dedicated assistance. We should think of formal mentoring as being on a continuum of care, falling somewhere between more intensive professional care and the informal support of a special teacher, aunt, or other natural mentor. As such, strategies that help youth to cultivate informal networks of support should be a staple of all mentoring programs—as an alternative to or transition from more intensive formal support. This will help to instill in youth the sense that they are entitled to the same mentoring opportunities as their more privileged peers, and that the skills for accessing and maintaining supportive networks can be learned and mastered. Indeed, it would be a mistake to be anything less than vigilant in supporting youth's access to the full continuum of effective relationships with caring adults.

Epilogue

Books and articles about mentoring often begin with a brief nod to Homer's epic poem *The Odyssey* to explain its etymology. In the poem, the legendary Greek king Odysseus asks his old friend Mentor to watch over his household and son Telemachus before leaving to fight in the Trojan War.[1] When the goddess Athena visits Telemachus, she appears in the form of Mentor so that she can provide help and guidance. The field of mentoring is a living tribute to Mentor, the personification of the protective, guiding, and supportive figures that we all deserve. This ancient myth neatly encapsulates our vision of the ideal intergenerational relationship and has helped to unify the thousands of programs as well as the eponymous organization MENTOR around common mentoring goals.

A closer reading of the poem, however, suggests that this field might have just as logically been named shepherd, seagull, ship captain's daughter, or swallow, all of which were forms that the Greek goddess Athena inhabited to dispense her wisdom.[2] Granted, Athena's first appearance was that of "a Taphian chieftain named Mentes," but Mentor was still by no means a major figure in this epic poem and provided very little in the way of support, protection, advice, or counsel to young Telemachus. Mentor actually allowed

Odysseus's household to sink into ruin and be overrun with unwanted suitors who bullied Telemachus and harassed his mother, Penelope. This is a far cry from the image of a wise and nurturing advisor.

We owe our archetypal notions of Mentor not to Homer's *Odyssey*, but to one of the most popular and subversive books of the seventeenth century, *Les aventures de Telemaque*, a French novel by Fénelon, archbishop of Cambrai and tutor to the Duke of Burgundy, who was the grandson of Louis XIV.[3] In recounting the original poem to his royal pupil, Fénelon took a fan-fiction writer's creative liberty, spinning it into a new tale of the educational travels of Telemachus and his tutor, Mentor. In doing so, the reframed novel became a scathing rebuke of the autocratic reign of the king, the excesses of wealth, and royal preferences for luxury at the expense of the everyday laborers. This reframing may help to account for both the enormous appeal it had and Fénelon's banishment from the court of Versailles.

As historian Andy Roberts and other scholars have argued, it was this book that precipitated the popular use of the term "mentor" to describe a caring, older adult. Indeed, although there had been no mention of the term "mentor" in the previous centuries, it came into common usage in the decades following the publication of this book. As Roberts notes:

> It is thanks to Fénelon, and the "age of enlightenment" that the modern-day allusions of the word mentor were brought into the language at all. It is thanks to Fénelon that the term mentor was resurrected from circa 1000 b.c. and brought into the language circa 1750 a.d., thus filling a gap of some three millennia. . . . It is Fénelon's Mentor, not Homer's, that should be referred to when

considering the popular environmental connotations that the word mentor now implies. Any reading of *The Odyssey* will not find such rich references to the character Mentor that counsels, guides, nurtures, advises and enables.[4]

It is perhaps fitting that our collective understanding of Mentor was built on a foundation of mythology and inaccuracy. It is also quite remarkable that so many of us tacitly accepted this mythical origin story when evidence to the contrary requires little more than a cursory read of the ancient poem. In much the same way, the disappointing verdicts on mentoring effectiveness that have been compiled in this book have been hiding in plain sight for decades. Yet misguided assumptions, high hopes, and confirmation biases prevented many in this field, including me, from internalizing their lessons and making the necessary corrections.

Fénelon's twist notwithstanding, *The Odyssey* does impart some valuable lessons about mentoring. First, there is the issue of Mentor's fallibility. Mentor himself may not have lived up to his mythology but his mortal imperfections suggest a more realistic understanding of the limits and complexities of the role. Exaggerated expectations for what mentors and programs can and should deliver have intimidated and dissuaded potential volunteers while minimizing the contributions of the many everyday caring adults and program staff members who, collectively, play a role in supporting youth development.

Additional wisdom appears in both the poem and in Fénelon's interpretation. In assuming so many different mentoring personas, Athena seemed to intuit that a single tree cannot possibly shade a child's path to adulthood. Many of us have had multiple and even concurrent mentors, from professional providers and formal mentors to people in our families and everyday lives. And finally, Fénelon's critiques of wealth concentration and his calls for economic justice remain as relevant today as they did under Louis XIV.

In a special issue of the *Journal of Primary Prevention* devoted to my mentor, George Albee, the editors wrote that

> George's way of helping people to develop is to invite them to "come along," . . . to walk with him in his path and to see the world through his lenses: a world free from exploitation and domination of one group by another, a world in which each person has the freedom and the resources to develop her or his potential to the fullest, a world in which the highest goal would be one person's concern and regard for others. As always, with George's invitation comes the unwritten command to fight the good fight . . . with energy, commitment, and enthusiasm.

If you've made it this far, I can only hope that, with a renewed resolve, you will be fighting the good fight to ensure a more promising future for all youth.

Notes

INTRODUCTION

1. A. Lareau, *Unequal Childhoods: Class, Race, and Family Life,* 2nd ed., with an update a decade later (Berkeley: University of California Press, 2011).

2. E. B. Raposa, N. Dietz, and J. E. Rhodes, "Trends in Volunteer Mentoring in the United States: Analysis of a Decade of Census Survey Data," *American Journal of Community Psychology* 59, no. 1–2 (2017): 1–12; J. B. Kupersmidt et al., "Predictors of Premature Match Closure in Youth Mentoring Relationships," *American Journal of Community Psychology* 59, no. 1–2 (2017): 25–35.

3. G. R. Jarjoura et al., *Evaluation of the Mentoring Enhancement Demonstration Program: Technical Report* (Washington, DC: American Institute for Research, 2018); Kupersmidt et al., "Predictors of Premature Match Closure."

4. Jarjoura et al., *Evaluation of the Mentoring Enhancement Demonstration Program.*

5. Jarjoura et al., *Evaluation of the Mentoring Enhancement Demonstration Program,* 177.

6. J. C. Norcross and M. J. Lambert, "The Therapy Relationship," in *Evidence-Based Practices in Mental Health: Debate and Dialogue on the Fundamental Questions* (Washington, DC: American Psychological Association, 2006), 208–218; B. E. Wampold, H.-n. Ahn, and

H. L. K. Coleman, "Medical Model as Metaphor: Old Habits Die Hard," *Journal of Counseling Psychology* 48, no. 3 (2001): 268-273.

7. T. A. Cavell and L. C. Elledge, "Mentoring and Prevention Science," in *Handbook of Youth Mentoring,* ed. D. L. DuBois and M. J. Karcher (Thousand Oaks, CA: SAGE, 2015), 29-42.

8. V. Sacks and D. Murphy, "The Prevalence of Adverse Childhood Experiences, Nationally, by State, and by Race and Ethnicity," Child Trends, 2018, https://www.childtrends.org/publications /prevalence-adverse-childhood-experiences-nationally-state-race -ethnicity.

9. Cavell and Elledge, "Mentoring and Prevention Science."

10. S. B. Heller et al., "Thinking, Fast and Slow? Some Field Experiments to Reduce Crime and Dropout in Chicago," *Quarterly Journal of Economics* 132, no. 1 (2017): 1-54.

11. J. M. Preston, Ò. Prieto-Flores, and J. E. Rhodes, "Mentoring in Context: A Comparative Study of Youth Mentoring Programs in the United States and Continental Europe," *Youth & Society* 51, no. 7 (2019): 900-914.

12. M. Garringer and C. Benning, *The Power of Relationships: How and Why American Adults Step Up to Mentor the Nation's Youth* (Boston: MENTOR, 2018); M. Hagler, S. McQuillin, and J. Rhodes, "Ideological Profiles of U.S. Adults and Their Support for Youth Mentoring," *Journal of Community Psychology* 48, no. 2 (2020): 209-224.

13. L. Van Dam et al., "Does Natural Mentoring Matter? A Multilevel Meta-analysis on the Association between Natural Mentoring and Youth Outcomes," *American Journal of Community Psychology* 62, no. 1-2 (2017): 203-220.

14. M. A. Hagler and J. E. Rhodes, "The Long-Term Impact of Natural Mentoring Relationships: A Counterfactual Analysis," *American Journal of Community Psychology* 62, no. 1-2 (2018): 175-188; M. A. Zimmerman, J. B. Bingenheimer, and D. E. Behrendt, "Natural

Mentoring Relationships," in *Handbook of Youth Mentoring*, 143–157; E. B. Raposa et al., "How Economic Disadvantage Affects the Availability and Nature of Mentoring Relationships during the Transition to Adulthood," *American Journal of Community Psychology* 61, no. 1–2 (2018): 191–203.

1. "THE KIND OF JUSTICE WHICH ONLY A BROTHER CAN GIVE"

1. Interview with Irving Westheimer, box 85, no. 5, Rm III Oral Histories, Dorot Jewish Division, New York City Public Library.
2. D. L. DuBois and M. J. Karcher, eds., *Handbook of Youth Mentoring* (Thousand Oaks, CA: SAGE, 2015).
3. E. K. Coulter, *The Children in the Shadow* (New York: McBride, Nast, 1913).
4. Coulter, *The Children in the Shadow*.
5. D. Baker and C. Maguire, "Mentoring in Historical Perspective," in *Handbook of Youth Mentoring*, 14–29.
6. Coulter, *The Children in the Shadow*.
7. H. S. Gurteen, *Handbook of Charity Organization* (Buffalo, NY: n.p., 1882); Baker and Maguire, "Mentoring in Historical Perspective."
8. Baker and Maguire, "Mentoring in Historical Perspective."
9. J. Lepore, *These Truths: A History of the United States* (New York: W. W. Norton, 2018).
10. E. Roosevelt, "What Ten Million Women Want," Social Welfare History Project, 1932, https://socialwelfare.library.vcu.edu/recent/page/51/.
11. T. Piketty and E. Saez, "The Evolution of Top Incomes: A Historical and International Perspective," *American Economic Review* 96, no. 2 (2006): 200–205.
12. G. Packer, *The Unwinding: An Inner History of the New America* (New York: Macmillan, 2014).
13. J. N. Albright, N. M. Hurd, and S. B. Hussain, "Applying a Social Justice Lens to Youth Mentoring: A Review of the Literature and

Recommendations for Practice," *American Journal of Community Psychology* 59, no. 3-4 (2017): 363-381; S. E. O. Schwartz and J. E. Rhodes, "From Treatment to Empowerment: New Approaches to Youth Mentoring," *American Journal of Community Psychology* 58, no. 1-2 (2016): 150-157.

14. M. Raz, *What's Wrong with the Poor? Psychiatry, Race, and the War on Poverty* (Chapel Hill: University of North Carolina Press, 2013).

15. See, for example, E. J. Green, W. T. Greenough, and B. E. Schlumpf, "Effects of Complex or Isolated Environments on Cortical Dendrites of Middle-Aged Rats," *Brain Research* 264, no. 2 (1983): 233-240.

16. Raz, *What's Wrong with the Poor?*

17. H. Colley, *Mentoring for Social Inclusion: A Critical Approach to Nurturing Mentor Relationships* (London: Routledge, 2003).

18. G. Walker, "Youth Mentoring and Public Policy," in *Handbook of Youth Mentoring,* 510-524.

19. J. P. Tierney, J. B. Grossman, and N. L. Resch, *Making a Difference: An Impact Study of Big Brothers Big Sisters* (Philadelphia: Public / Private Ventures, 1995).

20. J. E. Rhodes and D. L. DuBois, "Understanding and Facilitating the Youth Mentoring Movement," *Social Policy Report* 20, no. 3 (2006): 1-20.

21. J. McCord, "A Thirty-Year Follow-Up of Treatment Effects," *American Psychologist* 33, no. 3 (1978): 284-289.

22. Baker and Maguire, "Mentoring in Historical Perspective."

23. D. L. DuBois et al., "Effectiveness of Mentoring Programs for Youth: A Meta-analytic Review," *American Journal of Community Psychology* 30, no. 2 (2002): 157-197; Rhodes and DuBois, "Understanding and Facilitating the Youth Mentoring Movement."

24. J. B. Grossman and J. E. Rhodes, "The Test of Time: Predictors and Effects of Duration in Youth Mentoring Programs," *American Journal of Community Psychology* 30, no. 2 (2002): 199-206.

25. P. Dawson, "Beyond a Definition: Toward a Framework for Designing and Specifying Mentoring Models," *Educational Researcher* 43, no. 3 (2014): 137–145.

26. M. J. Karcher et al., "Mentoring Programs: A Framework to Inform Program Development, Research, and Evaluation," *Journal of Community Psychology* 34, no. 6 (2006): 709–725.

27. J. Preston, Ò. Prieto-Flores, and J. Rhodes, "Mentoring in Context: A Comparative Study of Youth Mentoring Programs in the United States and Continental Europe," *Youth & Society* 51, no. 7 (2019): 900–914.

28. D. L. DuBois and M. J. Karcher, "Youth Mentoring: Theory, Research, and Practice," in *Handbook for Youth Mentoring,* 2–11.

29. Walker, "Youth Mentoring and Public Policy."

30. A. L. Fernandes-Alcantara, *Vulnerable Youth: Federal Mentoring Programs and Issues,* CRS Report R34306 (Washington, DC: Congressional Research Service, 2015).

31. J. B. Grossman and E. M. Garry, *Mentoring—A Proven Delinquency Prevention Strategy* (Washington, DC: US Department of Justice, Office of Justice Programs, Office of Juvenile Justice and Delinquency Prevention, 1997).

32. G. R. Jarjoura et al., *Evaluation of the Mentoring Enhancement Demonstration Program: Technical Report* (Washington, DC: American Institute for Research, 2018).

33. DuBois et al., "Effectiveness of Mentoring Programs for Youth."

34. M. Freedman, *The Kindness of Strangers: Adult Mentors, Urban Youth, and the New Voluntarism* (Cambridge: Cambridge University Press, 1999).

35. K. Hansan and J. Corlett, *2006 Big Brothers Big Sisters School-Based Mentoring Survey Report* (Philadelphia: Big Brothers Big Sisters, 2006).

36. Rhodes and DuBois, "Understanding and Facilitating the Youth Mentoring Movement."

37. Baker and Maguire, "Mentoring in Historical Perspective."

2. MENTORING BY THE NUMBERS

1. J. M. Preston, Ò. Prieto-Flores, and J. E. Rhodes, "Mentoring in Context: A Comparative Study of Youth Mentoring Programs in the United States and Continental Europe," *Youth & Society* 51, no. 7 (2019): 900–914.

2. J. Cohen, *Statistical Power Analysis for the Behavioral Sciences* (Hillsdale, NJ: Lawrence Erlbaum Associates, Publishers, 1988).

3. E. E. Tanner-Smith, J. A. Durlak, and R. A. Marx, "Empirically Based Mean Effect Size Distributions for Universal Prevention Programs Targeting School-Aged Youth: A Review of Meta-analyses," *Prevention Science* 19, no. 8 (2018): 1091–1101.

4. J. B. Grossman and J. P. Tierney, "Does Mentoring Work?: An Impact Study of the Big Brothers Big Sisters Program," *Evaluation Review* 22, no. 3 (1998): 403–426; D. J. De Wit et al., "Feasibility of a Randomized Controlled Trial for Evaluating the Effectiveness of the Big Brothers Big Sisters Community Match Program at the National Level," *Children and Youth Services Review* 29, no. 3 (2007): 383–404; P. Dolan et al., *Big Brothers Big Sisters (BBBS) of Ireland: Evaluation Study* (Galway, Ireland: Child and Family Research Centre, 2010); C. Herrera, D. L. DuBois, and J. B. Grossman, *The Role of Risk: Mentoring Experiences and Outcomes for Youth with Varying Risk Profiles* (New York: MDRC, 2013).

5. J. E. Rhodes and D. L. DuBois, "Understanding and Facilitating the Youth Mentoring Movement," *Social Policy Report* 20, no. 3 (2006): 1–20.

6. J. M. Eddy et al., "A Randomized Controlled Trial of a Long-Term Professional Mentoring Program for Children at Risk: Outcomes across the First 5 Years," *Prevention Science* 18 (2017): 899–910.

7. C. Herrera et al., "Mentoring in Schools: An Impact Study of Big Brothers Big Sisters School-Based Mentoring," *Child Development* 82, no. 1 (2011): 346–361.

8. J. P. Tierney, J. P. Grossman, and N. L. Resch, "Making a Difference: An Impact Study of Big Brothers / Big Sisters," Issue Lab,

2000; C. Herrera, D. L. DuBois, and J. B. Grossman, *The Role of Risk: Mentoring Experiences and Outcomes for Youth with Varying Risk Profiles* (New York: Public / Private Ventures, 2013); D. De Wit et al., "Mentoring Relationships and the Well-Being of Canadian Youth: An Examination of Big Brothers Big Sisters Community Match Programs," Big Brothers Vancouver, June 13, 2014; Dolan et al., *Big Brothers Big Sisters of Ireland,* report 2.

9. A. W. Johnson, "Mentoring At-Risk Youth: A Research Review and Evaluation of the Impacts of the Sponsor-A-Scholar Program on Student Performance," *Dissertation Abstracts International Section A: Humanities and Social Sciences* 58, no. 3-A (1997): 0813; M. J. Karcher, C. Davis, and B. Powell, "The Effects of Developmental Mentoring on Connectedness and Academic Achievement," *School Community Journal* 12, no. 2 (2002): 35–50.

10. Karcher, Davis, and Powell, "The Effects of Developmental Mentoring on Connectedness and Academic Achievement"; J. F. Jent and L. N. Niec, "Mentoring Youth with Psychiatric Disorders: The Impact on Child and Parent Functioning," *Child and Family Behavior Therapy* 28, no. 3 (2006): 43–58; J.-A. Sowers et al., "A Randomized Trial of a Science, Technology, Engineering, and Mathematics Mentoring Program," *Career Development and Transition for Exceptional Individuals* 40, no. 4 (2017): 196–204.

11. K. A. King et al., "Increasing Self-Esteem and School Connectedness through a Multidimensional Mentoring Program," *Journal of School Health* 72, no. 7 (2002): 294–299.

12. T. A. Cavell and L. C. Elledge, "Mentoring and Prevention Science," in *Handbook of Youth Mentoring,* ed. D. L. DuBois and M. J. Karcher (Thousand Oaks, CA: SAGE, 2015), 29–42.

13. T. D. Little, *Longitudinal Structural Equation Modeling* (New York: Guilford Press, 2016).

14. A. K. Henneberger et al., "The Young Women Leaders Program: A Mentoring Program Targeted toward Adolescent Girls," *School Mental Health* 5, no. 3 (2013): 132–143. G. R. Jarjoura, *Evaluation*

Report: Aftercare for Indiana through Mentoring (Bloomington: Indiana University School of Public and Environmental Affairs, 2007).

15. D. L. DuBois et al., "How Effective Are Mentoring Programs for Youth?: A Systematic Assessment of the Evidence," *Psychological Science in the Public Interest* 12, no. 2 (2011): 57–91.

16. E. B. Raposa et al., "The Effects of Youth Mentoring Programs: A Meta-analysis of Outcome Studies," *Journal of Youth and Adolescence* 48, no. 3 (2019): 423–443.

17. D. Jolliffe and D. P. Farrington, *A Rapid Evidence Assessment of the Impact of Mentoring on Re-offending: A Summary* (Cambridge, UK: Home Office, 2007); P. Tolan et al., "Mentoring Interventions to Affect Juvenile Delinquency and Associated Problems: A Systematic Review," *Campbell Systematic Reviews* 9, no. 1 (2013): 1–158.

18. L. T. Eby et al., "Does Mentoring Matter?: A Multidisciplinary Meta-analysis Comparing Mentored and Non-mentored Individuals," *Journal of Vocational Behavior* 72, no. 2 (2008): 254–267.

19. D. L. DuBois et al., "Effectiveness of Mentoring Programs for Youth: A Meta-analytic Review," *American Journal of Community Psychology* 30, no. 2 (2002): 157–197.

20. Raposa et al., "The Effects of Youth Mentoring Programs."

21. DuBois et al., "Effectiveness of Mentoring Programs for Youth," 177.

22. Raposa et al., "The Effects of Youth Mentoring Programs."

23. Raposa et al., "The Effects of Youth Mentoring Programs."

24. K. Christensen et al., "Non-specific versus Targeted Approaches to Youth Mentoring: A Follow-Up Meta-analysis," *Journal of Youth and Adolescence* (under review).

25. "Benefit-Cost Results," Washington State Institute for Public Policy, 2019, http://www.wsipp.wa.gov/BenefitCost.

26. A. C. K. Cheung and R. E. Slavin, "How Methodological Features Affect Effect Sizes in Education," *Educational Researcher* 45, no. 5 (2016): 283–292.

27. Y. N. Alfonso et al., "A Marginal Cost Analysis of a Big Brothers Big Sisters of America Youth Mentoring Program: New Evidence Using Statistical Analysis," *Children and Youth Services Review* 101 (June 2019): 23-32.

28. M. Foster, "What We Know about the Cost-Effectiveness of Mentoring," *Social Policy Report* 34, no. 3 (2010): 23-24.

29. M. Foster, "What We Know about the Cost-Effectiveness of Mentoring."

30. R. H. Aseltine, M. Dupre, and P. Lamlein, "Mentoring as a Drug Prevention Strategy: An Evaluation of Across Ages," *Adolescent and Family Health* 1, no. 1 (2000): 11-20.

31. Johnson, "Mentoring At-Risk Youth."

32. L. Bernstein et al., *Impact Evaluation of the US Department of Education's Student Mentoring Program. Final Report,* NCEE 2009-4047 (Washington, DC: National Center for Education Evaluation and Regional Assistance, 2009).

33. N. Converse and B. Lignugaris-Kraft, "Evaluation of a School-Based Mentoring Program for At-Risk Middle School Youth," *Remedial and Special Education* 30, no. 1 (2009): 33-46; J. DeSocio et al., "Engaging Truant Adolescents: Results from a Multifaceted Intervention Pilot," *Preventing School Failure: Alternative Education for Children and Youth* 51, no. 3 (2007): 3-9; P. A. Wyman et al., "Intervention to Strengthen Emotional Self-Regulation in Children with Emerging Mental Health Problems: Proximal Impact on School Behavior," *Journal of Abnormal Child Psychology* 38, no. 5 (2010): 707-720.

34. A. M. January, R. J. Casey, and D. Paulson, "A Meta-analysis of Classroom-Wide Interventions to Build Social Skills: Do They Work?," *School Psychology Review* 40, no. 2 (2011): 242-256.

35. J. C. Norcross and M. J. Lambert, "The Therapy Relationship," in *Evidence-Based Practices in Mental Health: Debate and Dialogue on the Fundamental Questions* (Washington, DC: American Psychological Association, 2006), 208-218; B. E. Wampold, H.-n. Ahn, and

H. L. K. Coleman, "Medical Model as Metaphor: Old Habits Die Hard," *Journal of Counseling Psychology* 48, no. 3 (2001): 268–273.

36. For example, just a few years ago, Laska et al. noted that the "necessary and sufficient" conditions for all therapeutic change, irrespective of any additional techniques, were the nonspecific factors such as the bond, setting, plausible explanations, and positive expectations: K. M. Laska, A. S. Gurman, and B. E. Wampold, "Expanding the Lens of Evidence-Based Practice in Psychotherapy: A Common Factors Perspective," *Psychotherapy* 51, no. 4 (2014): 467–481.

37. T. Baker, R. McFall, and V. Shoham, "Is Your Therapist a Little Behind the Times?," *Washington Post,* November 15, 2009, 73.

38. J. R. Weisz et al., "Promoting and Protecting Youth Mental Health through Evidence-Based Prevention and Treatment," *American Psychologist* 60, no. 6 (2005): 628–648.

39. J. R. Weisz, A. J. Doss, and K. M. Hawley, "Youth Psychotherapy Outcome Research: A Review and Critique of the Evidence Base," *Annual Review of Psychology* 56 (2005): 337–363; J. R. Weisz et al., "Performance of Evidence-Based Youth Psychotherapies Compared with Usual Clinical Care: A Multilevel Meta-analysis," *JAMA Psychiatry* 70, no. 7 (2013); J. R. Weisz et al., "What Five Decades of Research Tells Us about the Effects of Youth Psychological Therapy: A Multilevel Meta-analysis and Implications for Science and Practice," *American Psychologist* 72, no. 2 (2017): 79–117.

40. Weisz, Doss, and Hawley, "Youth Psychotherapy Outcome Research."

41. Weisz, Doss, and Hawley, "Youth Psychotherapy Outcome Research."

42. Weisz, Doss, and Hawley, "Youth Psychotherapy Outcome Research."

43. Weisz et al., "Performance of Evidence-Based Youth Psychotherapies"; Weisz et al., "What Five Decades of Research Tells Us about the Effects of Youth Psychological Therapy."

44. Weisz et al., "What Five Decades of Research Tells Us about the Effects of Youth Psychological Therapy."

45. M. Garringer, S. McQuillin, and H. L. McDaniel, *Examining Youth Mentoring Services across America: Findings from the 2016 National Mentoring Program Survey* (Washington, DC: MENTOR, 2017).

46. E. B. Raposa, J. E. Rhodes, and C. Herrera, "The Impact of Youth Risk on Mentoring Relationship Quality: Do Mentor Characteristics Matter?," *American Journal of Community Psychology* 57, no. 3–4 (2016): 320–329.

47. J. Li and M. M. Julian, "Developmental Relationships as the Active Ingredient: A Unifying Working Hypothesis of 'What Works' across Intervention Settings," *American Journal of Orthopsychiatry* 82, no. 2 (2012): 157–166.

48. J. J. Heckman and T. Kautz, "Fostering and Measuring Skill: Interventions That Improve Character and Cognition," National Bureau of Economic Research, 2013, https://www.nber.org/papers/w19656.

49. J. E. Rhodes, "A Model of Youth Mentoring," in *Handbook of Youth Mentoring*, 30–43.

50. T. B. Smith and J. E. Trimble, "Culturally Adapted Mental Health Services: An Updated Meta-analysis of Client Outcomes," in *Foundations of Multicultural Psychology: Research to Inform Effective Practice* (Washington, DC: American Psychological Association, 2016), 129–144.

51. Weisz et al., "What Five Decades of Research Tells Us about the Effects of Youth Psychological Therapy."

52. M. J. Karcher, *Ten-Year Follow-Up on the RCT Study of Mentoring in the Learning Environment (SMILE): Effects of the Communities in Schools Mentoring Program on Crime and Educational Persistence*

(Washington, DC: US Department of Justice, Office of Justice Programs, 2019). This work won the Mentoring Research Best Practices Award (#2013-JU-FX-0008) from the US Office of Juvenile Justice and Delinquency Prevention.

53. J. McCord, "A Thirty-Year Follow-Up of Treatment Effects," *American Psychologist* 33, no. 3 (1978): 284–289; D. L. DuBois, C. Herrera, and E. Higley, "Investigation of the Reach and Effectiveness of a Mentoring Program for Youth Receiving Outpatient Mental Health Services," *Children and Youth Services Review* 91 (2018): 85–93.

54. Rhodes and DuBois, "Understanding and Facilitating the Youth Mentoring Movement."

55. D. J. Levinson, *The Seasons of a Man's Life* (New York: Ballantine Books, 1979).

3. HOW DID WE GET IT SO WRONG FOR SO LONG?

1. L. Sechrest et al., "Strength, and Integrity of Treatment: Some Neglected Problems in Evaluation Research," in *Evaluation Studies Review Annual,* ed. L. Sechrest (Beverly Hills, CA: SAGE, 1979).

2. J. A. Durlak and E. P. DuPre, "Implementation Matters: A Review of Research on the Influence of Implementation on Program Outcomes and the Factors Affecting Implementation," *American Journal of Community Psychology* 41, no. 3–4 (2008): 327–350.

3. D. L. DuBois et al., "How Effective Are Mentoring Programs for Youth?: A Systematic Assessment of the Evidence," *Psychological Science in the Public Interest* 12, no. 2 (2011): 57–91; J. Kupersmidt et al., "Predictors of Premature Match Closure in Youth Mentoring Relationships," *American Journal of Community Psychology* 59, no. 1–2 (2017): 25–35.

4. D. L. DuBois and T. E. Keller, "Investigation of the Integration of Supports for Youth Thriving into a Community-Based Mentoring Program," *Child Development* 88, no. 5 (2017): 1480–1491.

5. DuBois and Keller, "Investigation of the Integration of Supports for Youth Thriving into a Community-Based Mentoring Program."

6. T. Rose, *The End of Average: How We Succeed in a World That Values Sameness* (New York: Harper One, 2016).

7. R. S. Gordon Jr., "An Operational Classification of Disease Prevention," *Public Health Reports* 98, no. 2 (1983): 107–109.

8. "Bigger Impact 2022," Big Brothers Big Sisters of America and Big Brothers Big Sisters Federation, 2017, http://2022.bbbs.org/.

9. G. R. Jarjoura et al., *Evaluation of the Mentoring Enhancement Demonstration Program: Technical Report* (Washington, DC: American Institute for Research, 2018).

10. "About One-Third of U.S. Children Are Living with an Unmarried Parent," Pew Research Center, 2018; Kids Count Data Center, *The 2017 Kids Count Data Book* (Baltimore: Annie E. Casey Foundation, 2017).

11. Jarjoura et al., *Evaluation of the Mentoring Enhancement Demonstration Program*.

12. Children's Defense Fund, *The State of America's Children* (Washington, DC: Children's Defense Fund, 2014); Mental Health America, *2017 State of Mental Health in America* (Alexandria, VA: Mental Health America, 2017); National Center for Educational Statistics, *The Condition of Education* (Washington, DC: National Center for Educational Statistics, 2017), https://nces.ed.gov/pubsearch/pubsinfo.asp?pubid=2017144.

13. M. L. Danielson et al., "Prevalence of Parent-Reported ADHD Diagnosis and Associated Treatment among U.S. Children and Adolescents, 2016," *Journal of Clinical Child and Adolescent Psychology* 47, no. 2 (2018): 199–212.

14. A. Eisenhower, J. Blacher, and H. Bush, "Longitudinal Associations between Externalizing Problems and Student-Teacher Relationship Quality for Young Children with ASD," *Research in Autism Spectrum Disorders* 9 (2015): 163–173; E. B. Raposa, J. E.

Rhodes, and C. Herrera, "The Impact of Youth Risk on Mentoring Relationship Quality: Do Mentor Characteristics Matter?," *American Journal of Community Psychology* 57, no. 3–4 (2016): 320–329; Jarjoura et al., *Evaluation of the Mentoring Enhancement Demonstration Program.*

15. C. Herrera, D. L. DuBois, and J. B. Grossman, *The Role of Risk: Mentoring Experiences and Outcomes for Youth with Varying Risk Profiles* (New York: MDRC, 2013).

16. E. E. Tanner-Smith, J. A. Durlak, and R. A. Marx, "Empirically Based Mean Effect Size Distributions for Universal Prevention Programs Targeting School-Aged Youth: A Review of Meta-analyses," *Prevention Science* 19, no. 8 (2018): 1091–1101.

17. Tanner-Smith, Durlak, and Marx, "Empirically Based Mean Effect Size Distributions for Universal Prevention Programs Targeting School-Aged Youth."

18. J. L. Schleider and J. R. Weisz, "Little Treatments, Promising Effects?: Meta-analysis of Single-Session Interventions for Youth Psychiatric Problems," *Journal of the American Academy of Child and Adolescent Psychiatry* 56, no. 2 (2017): 107–115.

19. Tanner-Smith, Durlak, and Marx, "Empirically Based Mean Effect Size Distributions for Universal Prevention Programs Targeting School-Aged Youth."

20. E. B. Raposa et al., "The Effects of Youth Mentoring Programs: A Meta-analysis of Outcome Studies," *Journal of Youth and Adolescence* 48, no. 3 (2019): 423–443.

21. A. L. Vázquez and M. T. Villodas, "Racial / Ethnic Differences in Caregivers' Perceptions of the Need for and Utilization of Adolescent Psychological Counseling and Support Services," *Cultural Diversity and Ethnic Minority Psychology* 25, no. 3 (2019): 323–330.

22. M. Sourk, L. M. Weiler, and T. A. Cavell, "Risk, Support, and Reasons for Wanting a Mentor: Comparing Parents of Youth in Community versus School-Based Matches," *Child and Youth Services Review* 99, no. 3 (2019): 156–164.

23. B. L. Cook, C. L. Barry, and S. H. Busch, "Racial / Ethnic Disparity Trends in Children's Mental Health Care Access and Expenditures from 2002 to 2007," *Health Services Research* 48, no. 1 (2013): 129–149; P. W. Corrigan, B. G. Druss, and D. A. Perlick, "The Impact of Mental Illness Stigma on Seeking and Participating in Mental Health Care," *Psychological Science in the Public Interest* 15, no. 2 (2014): 37–70; Vázquez and Villodas, "Racial / Ethnic Differences in Caregivers' Perceptions of the Need for and Utilization of Adolescent Psychological Counseling and Support Services."

24. M. Alegría et al., "Removing Obstacles to Eliminating Racial and Ethnic Disparities in Behavioral Health Care," *Health Affairs (Project Hope)* 35, no. 6 (2016): 991–999; Vázquez and Villodas, "Racial / Ethnic Differences in Caregivers' Perceptions of the Need for and Utilization of Adolescent Psychological Counseling and Support Services."

25. Cook, Barry, and Busch, "Racial / Ethnic Disparity Trends in Children's Mental Health Care Access and Expenditures from 2002 to 2007"; A. F. Garland et al., "Racial and Ethnic Differences in Utilization of Mental Health Services among High-Risk Youths," *American Journal of Psychiatry* 25, no. 5–6 (2003): 491–507.

26. Vázquez and Villodas, "Racial / Ethnic Differences in Caregivers' Perceptions of the Need for and Utilization of Adolescent Psychological Counseling and Support Services."

27. Kupersmidt et al., "Predictors of Premature Match Closure in Youth Mentoring Relationships."

28. M. Garringer, S. McQuillin, and H. L. McDaniel, *Examining Youth Mentoring Services across America: Findings from the 2016 National Mentoring Program Survey* (Washington, DC: MENTOR, 2017).

29. Garringer, McQuillin, and McDaniel, *Examining Youth Mentoring Services across America*; M. J. Karcher, C. Herrera, and K. Hansen, "'I Dunno, What Do You Wanna Do?': Testing a Framework to Guide Mentor Training and Activity Selection," *New Directions for Youth Development* 2010, no. 126 (2010): 51–69.

30. Karcher, Herrera, and Hansen, "'I Dunno, What Do You Wanna Do?,'" 52.

31. Jarjoura et al., *Evaluation of the Mentoring Enhancement Demonstration Program*.

32. Jarjoura et al., *Evaluation of the Mentoring Enhancement Demonstration Program*; M. Bruce and J. Bridgeland, *The Mentoring Effect: Young People's Perspectives on the Outcomes and Availability of Mentoring* (Washington, DC: Civic Enterprises with Hart Research Associates for MENTOR, 2014); D. L. DuBois and N. Silverthorn, "Characteristics of Natural Mentoring Relationships and Adolescent Adjustment: Evidence from a National Study," *Journal of Primary Prevention* 26, no. 2 (2005): 69–92.

33. M. Freedman, *The Kindness of Strangers: Adult Mentors, Urban Youth, and the New Voluntarism* (Cambridge: Cambridge University Press, 1999).

34. D. Brooks, "The Golden Age of Bailing," *New York Times*, July 7, 2017, https://www.nytimes.com/2017/07/07/opinion/the-golden -age-of-bailing.html.

35. Kupersmidt et al., "Predictors of Premature Match Closure in Youth Mentoring Relationships."

36. Kupersmidt et al., "Predictors of Premature Match Closure in Youth Mentoring Relationships."

37. E. B. Raposa et al., "How Economic Disadvantage Affects the Availability and Nature of Mentoring Relationships during the Transition to Adulthood," *American Journal of Community Psychology* 61, no. 1–2 (2018): 191–203.

38. E. B. Raposa, N. Dietz, and J. E. Rhodes, "Trends in Volunteer Mentoring in the United States: Analysis of a Decade of Census Survey Data," *American Journal of Community Psychology* 59, no. 1–2 (2017): 1–12.

39. Herrera, DuBois, and Grossman, *The Role of Risk*.

40. R. Spencer, "'It's Not What I Expected': Mentoring Relationship Failures," *Journal of Adolescent Research* 22, no. 4 (2007): 331–354;

Spencer et al., "Breaking Up Is Hard to Do: A Qualitative Interview Study of How and Why Youth Mentoring Relationships End," *Youth & Society* 49, no. 4 (2017): 438–460.

41. S. W. Barford and W. J. Whelton, "Understanding Burnout in Child and Youth Care Workers," *Child and Youth Care Forum* 39, no. 4 (2010): 271–287; D. Haski-Leventhal and D. Bargal, "The Volunteer Stages and Transitions Model: Organizational Socialization of Volunteers," *Human Relations* 61, no. 1 (2008): 67–102; A. Papastylianou, M. Kaila, and M. Polychronopoulos, "Teachers' Burnout, Depression, Role Ambiguity and Conflict," *Social Psychology of Education* 12, no. 3 (2009): 295–314; K. Wilkerson and J. Bellini, "Intrapersonal and Organizational Factors Associated with Burnout among School Counselors," *Journal of Counseling and Development* 84, no. 4 (2006): 440–450.

42. Spencer, "'It's Not What I Expected.'"

43. Jarjoura et al., *Evaluation of the Mentoring Enhancement Demonstration Program.*

44. A. S. Masten and N. Garmezy, "Risk, Vulnerability, and Protective Factors in Developmental Psychopathology," in *Advances in Clinical Child Psychology* (Boston: Springer, 1985).

45. T. A. Cavell and L. C. Elledge, "Mentoring and Prevention Science," in *Handbook of Youth Mentoring,* ed. D. L. DuBois and M. J. Karcher (Thousand Oaks, CA: SAGE, 2015), 29–42; G. M. Walton and T. D. Wilson, "Wise Interventions: Psychological Remedies for Social and Personal Problems," *Psychological Review* 125, no. 5 (2018): 617–655; J. R. Weisz, A. J. Doss, and K. M. Hawley, "Youth Psychotherapy Outcome Research: A Review and Critique of the Evidence Base," *Annual Review of Psychology* 56 (2005): 337–363; Durlak and DuPre, "Implementation Matters"; A. Wandersman et al., "Bridging the Gap between Prevention Research and Practice: The Interactive Systems Framework for Dissemination and Implementation," *American Journal of Community Psychology* 41, no. 3–4 (2008): 171–181.

46. R. M. Lerner, E. M. Dowling, and P. M. Anderson, "Positive Youth Development: Thriving as the Basis of Personhood and Civil Society," *Applied Developmental Science* 7, no. 3 (2003): 172–180; R. M. Lerner, "Positive Youth Development: A View of the Issues," *Journal of Early Adolescence* 25, no. 1 (2005): 10–16; S. Lewin-Bizan, E. P. Bowers, and R. M. Lerner, "One Good Thing Leads to Another: Cascades of Positive Youth Development among American Adolescents," *Development and Psychopathology* 22, no. 4 (2010): 759–770; K. Pittman, M. Irby, and T. Ferber, "Unfinished Business: Further Reflections on a Decade of Promoting Youth," in *Trends in Youth Development* (Boston: Springer, 2001).

47. S. E. O. Schwartz and J. E. Rhodes, "From Treatment to Empowerment: New Approaches to Youth Mentoring," *American Journal of Community Psychology* 58, no. 1–2 (2016): 150–157.

48. B. J. Hirsch, N. L. Deutsch, and D. L. DuBois, *After-School Centers and Youth Development: Case Studies of Success and Failure* (Cambridge: Cambridge University Press, 2011).

49. N. M. Hurd et al., "Appraisal Support from Natural Mentors, Self-Worth, and Psychological Distress: Examining the Experiences of Underrepresented Students Transitioning through College," *Journal of Youth and Adolescence* 47, no. 5 (2018): 1100–1112.

50. P. Tolan et al., "Toward an Integrated Approach to Positive Development: Implications for Intervention," *Applied Developmental Science* 20, no. 3 (2016): 214–236.

51. P. Tolan et al., "Toward an Integrated Approach to Positive Development: Implications for Intervention."

52. R. F. Catalano et al., "Positive Youth Development in the United States: Research Findings on Evaluations of Positive Youth Development Programs," *Annals of the American Academy of Political and Social Science* 591 (2004): 98–124.

53. A. M. Freund and P. B. Baltes, "Life-Management Strategies of Selection, Optimization and Compensation: Measurement by Self-Report and Construct Validity," *Journal of Personality and*

Social Psychology 82 (2002): 642–662; Hirsch, Deutsch, and DuBois, *After-School Centers and Youth Development;* Lerner, "Positive Youth Development"; Tolan et al., "Toward an Integrated Approach to Positive Development."

54. Lerner, "Positive Youth Development."

55. M. W. Lipsey and D. B. Wilson, "Effective Intervention for Serious Juvenile Offenders," in *Serious and Violent Juvenile Offenders: Risk Factors and Successful Interventions,* ed. R. Loeber and D. P. Farrington (Thousand Oaks, CA: SAGE, 1998), 313–345; P. Tolan and N. Guerra, *What Works in Reducing Adolescent Violence: An Empirical Review of the Field* (Boulder, CO: Institute of Behavioral Science, 1994); Cavell and Elledge, "Mentoring and Prevention Science"; D. L. DuBois and M. J. Karcher, "Youth Mentoring: Theory, Research, and Practice," in *Handbook for Youth Mentoring,* 2–11; J. E. Rhodes, "A Model of Youth Mentoring," in *Handbook of Youth Mentoring,* 30–43, http://ir.obihiro.ac.jp/dspace/handle/10322/3933.

56. Tolan et al., "Toward an Integrated Approach to Positive Development."

57. Tolan et al., "Toward an Integrated Approach to Positive Development."

58. S. D. McQuillin et al., "Assessing the Impact of School-Based Mentoring: Common Problems and Solutions Associated with Evaluating Nonprescriptive Youth Development Programs," *Applied Developmental Science* (2018): 6.

59. S. D. McQuillin et al., "Assessing the Impact of School-Based Mentoring," 5–6.

60. S. D. McQuillin et al., "Assessing the Impact of School-Based Mentoring," 7.

61. D. L. DuBois et al., "Effectiveness of Mentoring Programs for Youth: A Meta-analytic Review," *American Journal of Community Psychology* 30, no. 2 (2002): 157–197.

62. Durlak and DuPre, "Implementation Matters," 342.

63. Durlak and DuPre, "Implementation Matters," 327–350.

64. Thomas C. Schelling, "The Life You Save May Be Your Own," in *Problems in Public Expenditure Analysis,* ed. Samuel B. Chase (Washington, DC: Brookings Institute, 1968).

65. T. Kogut and I. Ritov, "The 'Identified Victim' Effect: An Identified Group, or Just a Single Individual?," *Journal of Behavioral Decision Making* 18, no. 3 (2005): 157–167.

66. P. Bloom, *Against Empathy: The Case for Rational Compassion* (New York: Ecco Publishing, 2017).

67. P. Slovic, "If I Look at the Mass I Will Never Act: Psychic Numbing and Genocide," in *Emotions and Risky Technologies* (Dordrecht, the Netherlands: Springer, 2010), 37–59.

68. S. Epstein, "Integration of the Cognitive and the Psychodynamic Unconscious," *American Psychologist* 49 (1994): 709–724.

69. National Public Radio, "Spoiler Alert! The Psychology of Surprise Endings," Hidden Brain, December 3, 2018, https://www.npr.org /transcripts/661878959.

70. Weisz, Doss, and Hawley, "Youth Psychotherapy Outcome Research."

71. C. Tavris and E. Aronson, *Mistakes Were Made (but Not by Me): Why We Justify Foolish Beliefs, Bad Decisions, and Hurtful Acts* (New York: Houghton Mifflin Harcourt, 2008).

72. J. Kruger and D. Dunning, "Unskilled and Unaware of It: How Difficulties in Recognizing One's Own Incompetence Lead to Inflated Self-Assessments," *Journal of Personality and Social Psychology* 77, no. 6 (1999): 1121–1134.

73. A. Mahmoodi et al., "Equality Bias Impairs Collective Decision-Making across Cultures," *Proceedings of the National Academy of Sciences* 112, no. 12 (2015): 3835–3840.

74. V. Tseng, "The Uses of Research in Policy and Practice," *Sharing Child and Youth Development Knowledge* 26, no. 2 (2012): 6; M. I. Honig and C. Coburn, "Evidence-Based Decision Making in School District Central Offices: Toward a Policy and Research Agenda," *Educational Policy* 22, no. 4 (2008): 578–608.

75. C. Funk, "Mixed Messages about Public Trust in Science," *Issues in Science and Technology* 34, no. 1 (2017): 86–88.

76. W. Davies, "How Statistics Lost Their Power—And Why We Should Fear What Comes Next," *Guardian*, January 19, 2017, https://www.theguardian.com/politics/2017/jan/19/crisis-of-statistics-big-data-democracy.

77. A. S. Bryk, L. M. Gomez, and A. Grunow, "Getting Ideas into Action: Building Networked Improvement Communities in Education," *Carnegie Perspectives* (blog), Carnegie Foundation for the Advancement of Teaching, 2011, 5, https://files.eric.ed.gov/fulltext/ED517575.pdf; M. R. Goldfried, "On the Assumptions Underlying Therapy Change Principles," *Journal of Psychotherapy Integration* 24, no. 4 (2014): 275–279.

78. K. D. Strosahl and P. J. Robinson, "Adapting Empirically Supported Treatments in the Era of Integrated Care: A Roadmap for Success," *Clinical Psychology: Science and Practice* 25, no. 3 (2018): e12246.

79. S. B. Heller et al., "Thinking, Fast and Slow? Some Field Experiments to Reduce Crime and Dropout in Chicago," *Quarterly Journal of Economics* 132, no. 1 (2017): 1–54.

80. "Resource Library," Center on the Developing Child, Harvard University, 2018, https://developingchild.harvard.edu/resources/.

81. T. Baker, R. McFall, and V. Shoham, "Is Your Therapist a Little Behind the Times?," *Washington Post*, November 15, 2009, 73.

4. GIVING PSYCHOLOGY AWAY

1. G. W. Albee, "Conceptual Models and Manpower Requirements in Psychology," *American Psychologist* 23, no. 5 (1968): 317.

2. G. A. Miller, "Psychology as a Means of Promoting Human Welfare," *American Psychologist* 24, no. 12 (1969): 1074.

3. J. Rappaport, *Community Psychology: Values, Research, and Action* (New York: Harcourt School, 1977).

4. E. L. Cowen, "Help Is Where You Find It: Four Informal Helping Groups," *American Psychologist* 37, no. 4 (1982): 385–395.

5. R. Spencer and J. E. Rhodes, "A Counseling and Psychotherapy Perspective on Mentoring Relationships," in *Handbook of Youth Mentoring*, ed. D. L. DuBois and M. Karcher (Thousand Oaks, CA: SAGE), 118–132.

6. J. D. Frank and J. Frank, *Persuasion and Healing: A Comparative Study of Psychotherapy* (Baltimore: Johns Hopkins University Press, 1973).

7. E. B. Raposa, J. E. Rhodes, and C. Herrera, "The Impact of Youth Risk on Mentoring Relationship Quality: Do Mentor Characteristics Matter?," *American Journal of Community Psychology* 57, no. 3–4 (2016): 320–329; M. J. Karcher, M. J. Nakkula, and J. Harris, "Developmental Mentoring Match Characteristics: Correspondence between Mentors' and Mentees' Assessments of Relationship Quality," *Journal of Primary Prevention* 26, no. 2 (2005): 93–110.

8. L. M. Gutman and I. Schoon, "Preventive Interventions for Children and Adolescents," *European Psychologist* 20, no. 4 (2015): 231–241.

9. G. A. Aarons et al., "Evidence-Based Practice Implementation and Staff Emotional Exhaustion in Children's Services," *Behaviour Research and Therapy* 47 (2009): 954–960; "World Health Report 2010," World Health Organization, https://www.who.int/healthsystems/topics/financing/healthreport/whr_background/en/; J. R. Cummings, H. Wen, and B. G. Druss, "Improving Access to Mental Health Services for Youth in the United States," *Journal of American Medical Association* 309, no. 6 (2013): 553–554.

10. M. O'Connell, J. Morris, and M. Hoge, "Innovation in Behavioral Health Workforce Education," *Administration and Policy in Mental Health* 32 (2004): 131–165.

11. G. A. Aarons et al., "Evidence-Based Practice Implementation and Staff Emotional Exhaustion in Children's Services"; C. Glisson, D. Dukes, and P. Green, "The Effects of the ARC Organizational Intervention on Caseworker Turnover, Climate, and Culture in Children's Service Systems," *Child Abuse and Neglect* 30, no. 8 (2006): 855–880.

12. D. R. Singla et al., "Psychological Treatments for the World: Lessons from Low- and Middle-Income Countries," *Annual Review of Clinical Psychology* 13 (2017): 149–181.

13. J. A. Durlak, "Comparative Effectiveness of Paraprofessional and Professional Helpers," *Psychological Bulletin* 86, no. 1 (1979): 80–92.

14. Durlak, "Comparative Effectiveness of Paraprofessional and Professional Helpers," 6.

15. J. A. Durlak and L. A. Jason, "Preventive Programs for School-Aged Children and Adolescents," in *Prevention of Problems in Childhood: Psychological Research and Applications,* ed. Michael C. Roberts and Lizette Peterson (New York: Wiley, 1984), 536.

16. J. A. Hattie, C. F. Sharpley, and H. J. Rogers, "Comparative Effectiveness of Professional and Paraprofessional Helpers," *Psychological Bulletin* 95, no. 3 (1984): 534; J. S. Berman and N. C. Norton, "Does Professional Training Make a Therapist More Effective?," *Psychological Bulletin* 98, no. 2 (1985): 401.

17. M. L. Smith, G. V. Glass, and T. I. Miller, "Meta-analysis of Psychotherapy," *American Psychologist* 41 (1980): 165–180.

18. J. R. Weisz et al., "Effectiveness of Psychotherapy with Children and Adolescents: A Meta-analysis for Clinicians," *Journal of Consulting and Clinical Psychology* 55, no. 4 (1987): 542–549.

19. M. F. Giangreco, J. C. Suter, and M. B. Doyle, "Paraprofessionals in Inclusive Schools: A Review of Recent Research," *Journal of Educational and Psychological Consultation* 20, no. 1 (2010): 41–57.

20. A. Christensen and N. S. Jacobson, "Who (or What) Can Do Psychotherapy: The Status and Challenge of Nonprofessional Therapies," *Psychological Science* 5 (1994): 8–14.

21. A. E. Karlsruher, "The Influence of Supervision and Facilitative Conditions on the Psychotherapeutic Effectiveness of Nonprofessional and Professional Therapists," *American Journal of Community Psychology* 4 (1976): 145–154.

22. Durlak, "Comparative Effectiveness of Paraprofessional and Professional Helpers," 80.

23. Durlak, "Comparative Effectiveness of Paraprofessional and Professional Helpers."

24. K. D. Baker and R. A. Neimeyer, "Therapist Training and Client Characteristics as Predictors of Treatment Response to Group Therapy for Depression," *Psychotherapy Research* 13, no. 1 (2003): 135–151.

25. J. R. Weisz et al., "Effects of Psychotherapy with Children and Adolescents Revisited: A Meta-analysis of Treatment Outcome Studies," *Psychological Bulletin* 117, no. 3 (1995): 450–468.

26. J. R. Weisz et al., "Effects of Psychotherapy with Children and Adolescents Revisited."

27. E. C. Montgomery et al., "Can Paraprofessionals Deliver Cognitive-Behavioral Therapy to Treat Anxiety and Depressive Symptoms?," *Bulletin of the Menninger Clinic* 74, no. 1 (2010): 45–62.

28. P. C. A. M. den Boer et al., "Paraprofessionals for Anxiety and Depressive Disorders," *Cochrane Database of Systematic Reviews* 2 (2005): CD004688.

29. A. Barlow et al., "Paraprofessional-Delivered Home-Visiting Intervention for American Indian Teen Mothers and Children: 3-Year Outcomes from a Randomized Controlled Trial," *American Journal of Psychiatry* 172 (2015): 154–162; S. Y. Shire et al., "Hybrid Implementation Model of Community Partnered Early Intervention for Toddlers with Autism," *Journal of Child Psychology and Psychiatry* 58 (2017): 612–622.

30. C. T. Matsuzaka et al., "Task-Shifting Interpersonal Counseling for Depression: A Pragmatic Randomized Controlled Trial in Primary Care," *BMC Psychiatry* 17 (2017): 225.

31. C. S. Conley et al., "A Meta-analysis of Indicated Mental Health Prevention Programs for At-Risk Higher Education Students," *Journal of Counseling Psychology* 64, no. 2 (2017): 121–140.

32. Conley et al., "A Meta-analysis of Indicated Mental Health Prevention Programs for At-Risk Higher Education Students."

33. "World Health Report 2010"; S. K. Bearman, R. L. Schneiderman, and E. Zoloth, "Building an Evidence Base for Effective Supervision Practices: An Analogue Experiment of Supervision to Increase EBT Fidelity," *Administration and Policy in Mental Health and Mental Health Services Research* 44, no. 2 (2017): 293–307.

34. G. R. Jarjoura et al., *Evaluation of the Mentoring Enhancement Demonstration Program: Technical Report* (Washington, DC: American Institute for Research, 2018).

35. Jarjoura et al., *Evaluation of the Mentoring Enhancement Demonstration Program*.

36. D. L. DuBois et al., "Effectiveness of Mentoring Programs for Youth: A Meta-analytic Review," *American Journal of Community Psychology* 30, no. 2 (2002): 157–197; E. B. Raposa et al., "The Effects of Youth Mentoring Programs: A Meta-analysis of Outcome Studies," *Journal of Youth and Adolescence* 48, no. 3 (2019): 423–443.

37. "Benefit-Cost Results," Washington State Institute for Public Policy, 2019, http://www.wsipp.wa.gov/BenefitCost.

38. Raposa, Rhodes, and Herrera, "The Impact of Youth Risk on Mentoring Relationship Quality."

39. S. D. McQuillin and M. D. Lyons, "Brief Instrumental School-Based Mentoring for Middle School Students: Theory and Impact," *Advances in School Mental Health Promotion* 9, no. 2 (2016): 73–89.

40. T. B. Baker and R. M. McFall, "The Promise of Science-Based Training and Application in Psychological Clinical Science," *Psychotherapy* 51, no. 4 (2014): 483.

41. Singla et al., "Psychological Treatments for the World."

42. Singla et al., "Psychological Treatments for the World."

43. M. D. Lyons and S. D. McQuillin, "Risks and Rewards of School-Based Mentoring Relationships: A Reanalysis of the Student Mentoring Program Evaluation," *School Psychology Quarterly* 34, no. 1 (2019): 76–85.

44. W. Seekles et al., "Stepped Care for Depression and Anxiety: From Primary Care to Specialized Mental Health Care: A Randomised Controlled Trial Testing the Effectiveness of a Stepped Care Program among Primary Care Patients with Mood or Anxiety Disorders," *BMC Health Services Research* 9, no. 1 (2009): 90; M. Hagler, S. McQuillin, and J. Rhodes, "Paraprofessional Youth Mentoring: A Framework for Integrating Youth Mentoring with Helping Institutions and Professions" (under review).

45. A. Whitaker et al., "Cops and No Counselors: How the Lack of School Mental Health Staff Is Harming Students," American Civil Liberties Union, 2019, https://www.aclu.org/sites/default /files/field_document/030419-acluschooldisciplinereport.pdf.

46. Whitaker et al., "Cops and No Counselors."

47. M. S. Savitz-Romer et al., "Data-Driven School Counseling: The Role of the Research–Practice Partnership," *Professional School Counseling* 22, no. 1 (2018): 1–9. ; M. Hurwitz and J. Howell, "Estimating Causal Impacts of School Counselors with Regression Discontinuity Designs," *Journal of Counseling and Development* 92, no. 3 (2014): 316–327.

48. T. A. Poynton and R. T. Lapan, "Aspirations, Achievement, and School Counselors' Impact on the College Transition," *Journal of Counseling and Development* 95, no. 4 (2017): 369–377.

49. Whitaker et al., "Cops and No Counselors."

50. B. R. Ragins and A. K. Verbos, "Positive Relationships in Action: Relational Mentoring and Mentoring Schemas in the Workplace," in *Exploring Positive Relationships at Work: Building a Theoretical and Research Foundation*, ed. J. E. Dutton and B. R. Ragins (Mahwah, NJ: Lawrence Erlbaum Associations, 2007), 91–116; R. Ghosh and T. G. Reio Jr., "Career Benefits Associated with Mentoring for Mentors: A Meta-analysis," *Journal of Vocational Behavior* 83, no. 1 (2013): 106–116.

5. SPECIALIZED MENTORING

1. T. A. Cavell and L. C. Elledge, "Mentoring and Prevention Science," in *Handbook of Youth Mentoring,* ed. D. L. DuBois and M. J. Karcher (Thousand Oaks, CA: SAGE), 29–42.

2. Cavell and Elledge, "Mentoring and Prevention Science."

3. S. McQuillin et al., "Brief Instrumental School-Based Mentoring for First- and Second-Year Middle School Students: A Randomized Evaluation," *Journal of Community Psychology* 43, no. 7 (2015): 885–899.

4. M. Lynch et al., "Arches Transformative Mentoring Program: An Implementation and Impact Evaluation in New York City," Urban Institute, 2018, https://www.urban.org/sites/default/files /publication/96601/arches_transformative_mentoring_program .pdf.

5. J. F. Jent and L. N. Niec, "Mentoring Youth with Psychiatric Disorders: The Impact on Child and Parent Functioning," *Child and Family Behavior Therapy* 28, no. 3 (2006): 43–58.

6. M. J. Karcher, "The Cross-Age Mentoring Program (CAMP): A Developmental Intervention for Promoting Students' Connectedness across Grade Levels," *Professional School Counseling* 12, no. 2 (2008): 137–143.

7. A. Bayer, J. B. Grossman, and D. L. DuBois, "Using Volunteer Mentors to Improve the Academic Outcomes of Underserved Students: The Role of Relationships," *Journal of Community Psychology* 43, no. 4 (2015): 425.

8. Cavell and Elledge, "Mentoring and Prevention Science," 37.

9. C. S. Conley et al., "A Meta-analysis of the Impact of Universal and Indicated Technology-Delivered Interventions for Higher Education Students," *Prevention Science* 17 (2016): 659–678.

10. J. B. Grossman and J. E. Rhodes, "The Test of Time: Predictors and Effects of Duration in Youth Mentoring Programs," *American Journal of Community Psychology* 30, no. 2 (2002): 199–206; J. B. Grossman

et al., "The Test of Time in School-Based Mentoring: The Role of Relationship Duration and Re-matching on Academic Outcomes," *American Journal of Community Psychology* 49, no. 1–2 (2012): 43–54.

11. D. L. DuBois et al., "Effectiveness of Mentoring Programs for Youth: A Meta-analytic Review," *American Journal of Community Psychology* 30, no. 2 (2002): 157–197; D. L. DuBois et al., "How Effective Are Mentoring Programs for Youth?: A Systematic Assessment of the Evidence," *Psychological Science in the Public Interest* 12, no. 2 (2011): 57–91; E. B. Raposa et al., "How Economic Disadvantage Affects the Availability and Nature of Mentoring Relationships during the Transition to Adulthood," *American Journal of Community Psychology* 61, no. 1–2 (2018): 191–203.

12. E. B. Raposa et al., "The Effects of Youth Mentoring Programs: A Meta-analysis of Outcome Studies," *Journal of Youth and Adolescence* 48, no. 3 (2019): 423–443.

13. Grossman et al., "The Test of Time in School-Based Mentoring."

14. M. Garringer, S. McQuillin, and H. L. McDaniel, *Examining Youth Mentoring Services across America: Findings from the 2016 National Mentoring Program Survey* (Washington, DC: MENTOR, 2017); L. Bernstein et al., "Impact Evaluation of the U. S. Department of Education's Student Mentoring Program. Final Report," Education Resources Information Center, 2009, https://eric.ed.gov/?id=ED504310.

15. McQuillin et al., "Brief Instrumental School-Based Mentoring for First- and Second-Year Middle School Students."

16. S. McQuillin, G. Straight, and E. Saeki, "Program Support and Value of Training in Mentors' Satisfaction and Anticipated Continuation of School-Based Mentoring Relationships," *Mentoring and Tutoring: Partnership in Learning* 23, no. 2 (2015): 133–148.

17. Jent and Niec, "Mentoring Youth with Psychiatric Disorders."

18. M. Wheeler, T. Keller, and D. L. DuBois, "Review of Three Recent Randomized Trials of School-Based Mentoring," *Social Policy Report* 24 (2010): 1–21.

19. S. D. McQuillin and M. D. Lyons, "Brief Instrumental School-Based Mentoring for Middle School Students: Theory and Impact," *Advances in School Mental Health Promotion* 9, no. 2 (2016): 73-89.

20. H. A. Valantine and F. S. Collins, "National Institutes of Health Addresses the Science of Diversity," *Proceedings of the National Academy of Sciences* 112, no. 40 (2015): 12240-12242.

21. D. D. Embry and A. Biglan, "Evidence-Based Kernels: Fundamental Units of Behavioral Influence," *Clinical Child and Family Psychology Review* 11, no. 3 (2008): 75-113.

22. T. H. Ollendick et al., "Comorbidity as a Predictor and Moderator of Treatment Outcome in Youth with Anxiety, Affective, Attention Deficit / Hyperactivity Disorder, and Oppositional / Conduct Disorders," *Clinical Psychology Review* 28, no. 8 (2008): 1447-1471.

23. L. K. Marchette and J. R. Weisz, "Practitioner Review: Empirical Evolution of Youth Psychotherapy toward Transdiagnostic Approaches," *Journal of Child Psychology and Psychiatry* 58, no. 9 (2017): 970-984.

24. Grossman et al., "The Test of Time in School-Based Mentoring."

25. A. M. January, R. J. Casey, and D. Paulson, "A Meta-analysis of Classroom-Wide Interventions to Build Social Skills: Do They Work?," *School Psychology Review* 40, no. 2 (2011): 242-256.

26. January, Casey, and Paulson, "A Meta-analysis of Classroom-Wide Interventions to Build Social Skills."

27. C. S. Conley et al., "A Meta-analysis of Indicated Mental Health Prevention Programs for At-Risk Higher Education Students," *Journal of Counseling Psychology* 64, no. 2 (2017): 121-140.

28. C. S. Conley et al., "A Meta-analysis of Indicated Mental Health Prevention Programs for At-Risk Higher Education Students."

29. D. C. Gottfredson et al., "Standards of Evidence for Efficacy, Effectiveness, and Scale-Up Research in Prevention Science: Next Generation," *Prevention Science* 16, no. 7 (2015): 893-926.

30. C. Conley, J. Durlak, and A. Kirsch, "A Meta-analysis of Universal Mental Health Prevention Programs for Higher Education Students," *Prevention Science* 16, no. 4 (2015): 487–507.

31. Conley, Durlak, and Kirsch, "A Meta-analysis of Universal Mental Health Prevention Programs for Higher Education Students," 489.

6. THE PROMISE OF EMBEDDED AND BLENDED MENTORING

1. M. Freedman, *How to Live Forever: The Enduring Power of Connecting the Generations* (New York: Public Affairs, 2018).

2. S. E. O. Schwartz and J. E. Rhodes, "From Treatment to Empowerment: New Approaches to Youth Mentoring," *American Journal of Community Psychology* 58, no. 1–2 (2016): 150–157.

3. "Leading with Experience: Engaging Older Adults as Community Leaders," Experience Corps, http://www.maineservice commission.gov/media/publications/old/C.3.%20Leading%20 with%20Experience.pdf. Accessed July 20, 2019.

4. M. C. Carlson et al., "Evidence for Neurocognitive Plasticity in At-Risk Older Adults: The Experience Corps Program," *Journals of Gerontology Series A: Biomedical Sciences and Medical Sciences* 64, no. 12 (2009): 1275–1282.

5. L. P. Fried et al., "Experience Corps: A Dual Trial to Promote the Health of Older Adults and Children's Academic Success," *Contemporary Clinical Trials* 36, no. 1 (2013): 1–13.

6. S. B. Heller et al., "Thinking, Fast and Slow? Some Field Experiments to Reduce Crime and Dropout in Chicago," *Quarterly Journal of Economics* 132, no. 1 (2017): 1–54.

7. D. Bornstein, "How a Tapestry of Care Helps Teens Succeed," *New York Times,* March 15, 2016, https://opinionator.blogs.nytimes.com /2016/03/15/how-a-tapestry-of-care-helps-teens-succeed/.

8. H. Bath, "Calming Together: The Pathway to Self Control," *Reclaiming Children and Youth* 16, no. 4 (2008): 44–46; H. N. Taussig and S. E. Culhane, "Impact of a Mentoring and Skills Group

Program on Mental Health Outcomes for Maltreated Children in Foster Care," *Archives of Pediatrics and Adolescent Medicine* 164, no. 8 (2010): 739–746; H. N. Taussig et al., "RCT of a Mentoring and Skills Group Program: Placement and Permanency Outcomes for Foster Youth," *Pediatrics* 130, no. 1 (2012): e33–39; M. Walkley and L. Cox, "Building Trauma-Informed Schools and Communities," *Children and Schools* 35, no. 2 (2013): 123–126.

9. L. Leenarts et al., "Evidence-Based Treatments for Children with Trauma-Related Psychopathology as a Result of Childhood Maltreatment: A Systematic Review," *European Child and Adolescent Psychiatry* 22, no. 5 (2013): 269–283.

10. S. D. McQuillin et al., "Strengthening and Expanding Child Services in Low Resource Communities: The Role of Task-Shifting and Just-in-Time Training," *American Journal of Community Psychology* 63, no. 3–4 (2019): 355–365.

11. F. Sacco, N. Pike, and J. K. Bourque, "Therapeutic Mentoring: Mentalization Training in the Community," *International Journal of Applied Psychoanalytic Studies* 11, no. 2 (2014): 138–150.

12. R. Jarjoura, *Indiana's Juvenile Reentry Program: Aftercare for Indiana through Mentoring (AIM)* (Indianapolis, IN: Aftercare for Indiana through Mentoring, 2005).

13. S. E. O. Schwartz et al., "Youth Initiated Mentoring: Investigating a New Approach to Working with Vulnerable Adolescents," *American Journal of Community Psychology* 52, no. 1 / 2 (2013): 155–169; M. Millenky, S. E. O. Schwartz, and J. E. Rhodes, "Supporting the Transition to Adulthood among High School Dropouts: An Impact Study of the National Guard Youth Challenge Program," *Prevention Science* 15 (2013): 448–459.

14. S. Castrechini and R. A. London, *Positive Student Outcomes in Community Schools* (Washington, DC: Center for American Progress, 2012); J. Epstein, *School, Family, and Community Partnerships, Student Economy Edition: Preparing Educators and Improving Schools* (New York: Routledge, 2018); J. Oakes, A. Maier, and

J. Daniel, *Community Schools: An Evidence-Based Strategy for Equitable School Improvement* (Boulder, CO: National Education Policy Center, 2017); M. E. Walsh et al., "A New Model for Student Support in High-Poverty Urban Elementary Schools: Effects on Elementary and Middle School Academic Outcomes," *American Educational Research Journal* 51, no. 4 (2014): 704–737.

15. Walsh et al., "A New Model for Student Support in High-Poverty Urban Elementary Schools."

16. "City Connects: Intervention and Impact Progress Report 2018," Trustees of Boston College, https://www.bc.edu/content/dam/bc1 /schools/lsoe/sites/coss/pdfs/CityConnectsProgressReport2018 .pdf.

17. L. M. Gutman and I. Schoon, "Preventive Interventions for Children and Adolescents," *European Psychologist* 20, no. 4 (2015): 231–241.

18. J. P. Shonkoff et al., "The Lifelong Effects of Early Childhood Adversity and Toxic Stress," *Pediatrics* 129, no. 1 (2012): e232–e246; J. A. Durlak, R. P. Weissberg, A. B. Dymnicki, R. D. Taylor, and K. Schellinger. "The Impact of Enhancing Students' Social and Emotional Learning: A Meta-analysis of School-Based Universal Interventions," *Child Development* 82, (2011): 405–432.

19. G. W. Ladd and J. Mize, "A Cognitive–Social Learning Model of Social-Skill Training," *Psychological Review* 90, no. 2 (1983): 127; R. P. Weissberg, M. Z. Caplan, and P. J. Sivo, "A New Conceptual Framework for Establishing School-Based Social Competence Promotion Programs" in *Primary Prevention of Psychopathology, Vol. 12. Primary Prevention and Promotion in the Schools,* ed. L. A. Bond and B. E. Compas (Newbury Park, CA: SAGE, 1989), 255–296.

20. M. M. McKay and W. M. Bannon Jr., "Engaging Families in Child Mental Health Services," *Child and Adolescent Psychiatric Clinics* 13, no. 4 (2004): 905–921; D. Wood, R. Kaplan, and V. C. McLoyd, "Gender Differences in the Educational Expectations of Urban, Low-Income African American Youth: The Role of Parents and

the School," *Journal of Youth and Adolescence* 36, no. 4 (2007): 417–427.

21. M. J. Baker-Ericzén, M. M. Jenkins, and R. Haine-Schlagel, "Therapist, Parent, and Youth Perspectives of Treatment Barriers to Family-Focused Community Outpatient Mental Health Services," *Journal of Child and Family Studies* 22, no. 6 (2013): 854–868.

22. A. M. January, R. J. Casey, and D. Paulson, "A Meta-analysis of Classroom-Wide Interventions to Build Social Skills: Do They Work?," *School Psychology Review* 40, no. 2 (2011): 242–256.

23. Center for Promise, *Don't Quit on Me: What Young People Who Left School Say about the Power of Relationships* (Washington, DC: America's Promise Alliance, 2015).

24. Y. N. Alfonso et al., "A Marginal Cost Analysis of a Big Brothers Big Sisters of America Youth Mentoring Program: New Evidence Using Statistical Analysis," *Children and Youth Services Review* 101 (2019): 23–32.

25. L. Marsch, S. Lord, and J. Dallery, *Behavioral Healthcare and Technology: Using Science-Based Innovations to Transform Practice* (New York: Oxford University Press, 2014); J. Firth et al., "The Efficacy of Smartphone-Based Mental Health Interventions for Depressive Symptoms: A Meta-analysis of Randomized Controlled Trials," *World Psychiatry* 16, no. 3 (2017): 287–298.

26. A. E. Kazdin and S. L. Blase, "Rebooting Psychotherapy Research and Practice to Reduce the Burden of Mental Illness," *Perspectives on Psychological Science* 6, no. 1 (2011): 21–37.

27. J. Torous et al., "Clinical Review of User Engagement with Mental Health Smartphone Apps: Evidence, Theory and Improvements," *Evidence-Based Mental Health* 21, no. 3 (2018): 116–119.

28. G. Andersson and P. Cuijpers, "Internet-Based and Other Computerized Psychological Treatments for Adult Depression: A Meta-analysis," *Cognitive Behaviour Therapy* 38, no. 4 (2009): 196–205; S. Perini, N. Titov, and G. Andrews, "Clinician-Assisted

Internet-Based Treatment Is Effective for Depression: Random-ized Controlled Trial," *Australian and New Zealand Journal of Psychiatry* 43, no. 6 (2009): 571–578.

29. M. Anderson and J. Jiang, "Teens, Social Media & Technology 2018," Pew Research Center, May 31, 2018, https://www.pew research.org/internet/2018/05/31/teens-social-media-technology -2018/.

30. R. Mojtabai et al., "Barriers to Mental Health Treatment: Results from the National Comorbidity Survey Replication," *Psychological Medicine* 41, no. 8 (2011): 1751–1761.

31. D. Bakker et al., "Mental Health Smartphone Apps: Review and Evidence-Based Recommendations for Future Developments," *JMIR Mental Health* 3, no. 1 (March 2016): e7.

32. Bakker et al., "Mental Health Smartphone Apps"; J. Nicholas et al., "Mobile Apps for Bipolar Disorder: A Systematic Review of Features and Content Quality," *Journal of Medical Internet Research* 17, no. 8 (2015): e198.

33. R. F. Muñoz, "Using Evidence-Based Internet Interventions to Reduce Health Disparities Worldwide," *Journal of Medical Internet Research* 12, no. 5 (2010): e60.

34. D. Mohr, P. Cuijpers, and K. Lehman, "Supportive Accountability: A Model for Providing Human Support to Enhance Adherence to eHealth Interventions," *Journal of Medical Internet Research* 13, no. 1 (2011): e30.

35. J. A. M. Flett et al., "Mobile Mindfulness Meditation: A Ran-domised Controlled Trial of the Effect of Two Popular Apps on Mental Health," *Mindfulness* 10, no. 5 (2019): 863–876; M. Econo-mides et al., "Improvements in Stress, Affect, and Irritability Following Brief Use of a Mindfulness-Based Smartphone App: A Randomized Controlled Trial," *Mindfulness* 9, no. 5 (2018): 1584–1593.

36. A. M. Roepke et al., "Randomized Controlled Trial of SuperBetter, a Smartphone-Based / Internet-Based Self-Help Tool to Reduce

Depressive Symptoms," *Games for Health Journal* 4, no. 3 (2015): 235–246.

37. Bakker et al., "Mental Health Smartphone Apps."

38. C. Stiles-Shields et al., "What Might Get in the Way: Barriers to the Use of Apps for Depression," *Digital Health* 3 (2017); E. G. Lattie et al., "Uptake and Usage of IntelliCare: A Publicly Available Suite of Mental Health and Well-Being Apps," *Internet Interventions* 4 (2016): 152–158.

39. S. M. Schueller, K. N. Tomasino, and D. C. Mohr, "Integrating Human Support into Behavioral Intervention Technologies: The Efficiency Model of Support," *Clinical Psychology: Science and Practice* 24, no. 1 (2017): 27–45.

40. Andersson and Cuijpers, "Internet-Based and Other Computerized Psychological Treatments for Adult Depression"; Mohr, Cuijpers, and Lehman, "Supportive Accountability"; V. Spek et al., "Internet-Based Cognitive Behaviour Therapy for Symptoms of Depression and Anxiety: A Meta-analysis," *Psychological Medicine* 37, no. 3 (2007): 319–328; M. G. Newman et al., "A Review of Technology-Assisted Self-Help and Minimal Contact Therapies for Anxiety and Depression: Is Human Contact Necessary for Therapeutic Efficacy?," *Clinical Psychology Review* 31, no. 1 (2011): 89–103.

41. N. Titov et al., "Transdiagnostic Internet Treatment for Anxiety and Depression: A Randomised Controlled Trial," *Behaviour Research and Therapy* 49, no. 8 (2011): 441–452.

42. C. Conley, J. Durlak, and A. Kirsch, "A Meta-analysis of Universal Mental Health Prevention Programs for Higher Education Students," *Prevention Science* 16, no. 4 (2015): 487–507.

43. Conley, Durlak, and Kirsch, "A Meta-analysis of Universal Mental Health Prevention Programs for Higher Education Students."

44. N. Titov et al., "Internet Treatment for Depression: A Randomized Controlled Trial Comparing Clinician vs. Technician Assistance," *PloS One* 5, no. 6 (2010): e10939.

45. Mohr, Cuijpers, and Lehman, "Supportive Accountability."

46. G. Bernal, M. I. Jiménez-Chafey, and M. M. Domenech Rodríguez, "Cultural Adaptation of Treatments: A Resource for Considering Culture in Evidence-Based Practice," *Professional Psychology: Research and Practice* 40, no. 4 (2009): 361; J. Torous et al., "Mental Health Mobile Phone App Usage, Concerns, and Benefits among Psychiatric Outpatients: Comparative Survey Study," *JMIR Mental Health* 5, no. 4 (2018): e11715.

47. N. Titov, "Internet-Delivered Psychotherapy for Depression in Adults," *Current Opinion in Psychiatry* 24, no. 1 (2011): 18–23.

48. Schueller, Tomasino, and Mohr, "Integrating Human Support into Behavioral Intervention Technologies."

49. Schueller, Tomasino, and Mohr, "Integrating Human Support into Behavioral Intervention Technologies."

50. A. Barak et al., "A Comprehensive Review and a Meta-analysis of the Effectiveness of Internet-Based Psychotherapeutic Interventions," *Journal of Technology in Human Services* 26, no. 2–4 (2008): 109–160; M. E. Larsen et al., "Using Science to Sell Apps: Evaluation of Mental Health App Store Quality Claims," *Nature Digital Medicine* 2 (2019): 18.

51. J. Linardon et al., "The Efficacy of App-Supported Smartphone Interventions for Mental Health Problems: A Meta-analysis of Randomized Controlled Trials," *World Psychiatry* 18, no. 3 (2019): 325–336.

52. Barak et al., "A Comprehensive Review and a Meta-analysis of the Effectiveness of Internet-Based Psychotherapeutic Interventions."

53. D. R. Singla et al., "Psychological Treatments for the World: Lessons from Low- and Middle-Income Countries," *Annual Review of Clinical Psychology* 13 (2017): 149–181.

54. M. S. Karver et al., "Meta-analysis of the Prospective Relation between Alliance and Outcome in Child and Adolescent Psychotherapy," *Psychotherapy* 55, no. 4 (2018): 341.

55. S. A. Baldwin and Z. E. Imel, "Therapist Effects: Findings and Methods," in *Bergin and Garfield's Handbook of Psychotherapy and Behavior Change,* ed. M. J. Lambert, 6th ed. (New York: Wiley, 2013), 258–297.

56. R. Spencer, "A Working Model of Mentors' Contributions to Youth Mentoring Relationship Quality: Insights from Research on Psychotherapy," *LEARNing Landscapes* 5 (2012): 295–312.

7. THE GOOD ENOUGH MENTOR

1. J. M. Gottman, "Gottman Couples Therapy," in *Clinical Handbook of Couple Therapy* (New York: Guilford Press, 2015), 129–157.

2. J. Pryce et al., "Mentoring in the Social Context: Mentors' Experiences with Mentees' Peers in a Site-Based Program," *Children and Youth Services Review* 56 (2015): 85–192; T. E. Keller and J. M. Pryce, "Mutual but Unequal: Mentoring as a Hybrid of Familiar Relationship Roles," *New Directions for Youth Development* 2010, no. 126 (2010): 33–50.

3. E. S. Bordin, "The Generalizability of the Psychoanalytic Concept of the Working Alliance," *Psychotherapy: Theory, Research, and Practice* 16 (1979): 252–260.

4. A. O. Horvath et al., "Alliance in Individual Psychotherapy," *Psychotherapy* 48, no. 1 (2011): 9.

5. G. S. Tryon and G. Winograd, "Goal Consensus and Collaboration," *Psychotherapy* 48, no. 1 (2011): 50–57.

6. S. Zilcha-Mano, "Is the Alliance Really Therapeutic?: Revisiting This Question in Light of Recent Methodological Advances," *American Psychologist* 72, no. 4 (2017): 311–325.

7. S. Carrell and B. Sacerdote, "Why Do College Going Interventions Work?," *American Economic Journal: Applied Economics* 9, no. 3 (2017): 124–151.

8. M. D. Lyons and S. D. McQuillin, "Risks and Rewards of School-Based Mentoring Relationships: A Reanalysis of the Student Mentoring Program Evaluation," *School Psychology Quarterly* 34,

no. 1 (2019): 76–85; A. Bayer, J. B. Grossman, and D. L. DuBois, "Using Volunteer Mentors to Improve the Academic Outcomes of Underserved Students: The Role of Relationships," *Journal of Community Psychology* 43, no. 4 (2015): 408–429.

9. T. B. Baker, R. M. McFall, and V. Shoham, "Current Status and Future Prospects of Clinical Psychology: Toward a Scientifically Principled Approach to Mental and Behavioral Health Care," *Psychological Science in the Public Interest* 9, no. 2 (2008): 67–103.

10. M. D. Lyons, S. D. McQuillin, and L. J. Henderson, "Finding the Sweet Spot: Investigating the Effects of Relationship Closeness and Instrumental Activities in School-Based Mentoring," *American Journal of Community Psychology* 63, no. 1–2 (2018): 1–11.

11. T. E. Keller and J. Pryce, "Different Roles and Different Results: How Activity Orientations Correspond to Relationship Quality and Student Outcomes in School-Based Mentoring," *Journal of Primary Prevention* 33, no. 1 (2012): 47.

12. M. D. Clark, "Strength-Based Practices—The ABC's of Working with Adolescents Who Don't Want to Work with You," *Federal Probation* 62 (1998): 46–53; M. S. Karver et al., "Meta-analysis of the Prospective Relation between Alliance and Outcome in Child and Adolescent Psychotherapy," *Psychotherapy* 55, no. 4 (2018): 341.

13. S. M. Ormhaug, T. K. Jensen, T. Wentzel-Larsen, and S. R Shirk. "The Therapeutic Alliance in Treatment of Traumatized Youths: Relation to Outcome in a Randomized Clinical Trial," *Journal of Consulting and Clinical Psychology* 82, no. 1 (2002): 52–64.

14. Lyons and McQuillin, "Risks and Rewards of School-Based Mentoring Relationships"; J. B. Grossman and J. E. Rhodes, "The Test of Time: Predictors and Effects of Duration in Youth Mentoring Programs," *American Journal of Community Psychology* 30 (2002): 199–206.

15. J. P. Allen, S. T. Hauser, and E. Borman-Spurrell, "Attachment Theory as a Framework for Understanding Sequelae of Severe

Adolescent Psychopathology: An 11-Year Follow-Up Study," *Journal of Consulting and Clinical Psychology* 64, no. 2 (1996): 254–263.

16. C. H. Cooley, "The Looking-Glass Self," in *Social Theory: The Multicultural and Classic Readings*, ed. C. Lemert (Boulder, CO: Westview, 2010).

17. G. H. Mead, *Mind, Self and Society from the Standpoint of a Social Behaviorist*, ed. C. W. Morris (Chicago: University of Chicago Press, 1934); H. Blumer, "Mead and Blumer: The Convergent Methodological Perspectives of Social Behaviorism and Symbolic Interactionism," *American Sociological Review* 45, no. 1 (1980): 409–419.

18. N. M. Hurd et al., "Appraisal Support from Natural Mentors, Self-Worth, and Psychological Distress: Examining the Experiences of Underrepresented Students Transitioning through College," *Journal of Youth and Adolescence* 47, no. 5 (2018): 1100–1112.

19. M. J. Karcher et al., "Pygmalion in the Program: The Role of Teenage Peer Mentors' Attitudes in Shaping Their Mentees' Outcomes," *Applied Developmental Science* 14 (2010): 212–227.

20. Karver et al., "Meta-analysis of the Prospective Relation between Alliance and Outcome in Child and Adolescent Psychotherapy."

21. C. J. Dalenberg et al., "Reality versus Fantasy: Reply to Lynn et al. (2014)," *Psychological Bulletin* 140, no. 3 (2014): 911–920.

22. E. Jung et al., "Perceived Therapist Genuineness Predicts Therapeutic Alliance in Cognitive Behavioural Therapy for Psychosis," *British Journal of Clinical Psychology* 54, no. 1 (2015): 34–48; M. Larsson et al., "Initial Motives and Organizational Context Enabling Female Mentors' Engagement in Formal Mentoring—A Qualitative Study from the Mentors' Perspective," *Children and Youth Services Review* 71 (2016): 17–26; R. Spencer, "Understanding the Mentoring Process between Adolescents and Adults," *Youth & Society* 37, no. 3 (2006): 287–315.

23. M. J. Karcher, C. Herrera, and K. Hansen, "'I Dunno, What Do You Wanna Do?': Testing a Framework to Guide Mentor Training

and Activity Selection," *New Directions for Youth Development* 2010, no. 126 (2010): 51–69; S. D. McQuillin et al., "Strengthening and Expanding Child Services in Low Resource Communities: The Role of Task-Shifting and Just-in-Time Training," *American Journal of Community Psychology* 63, no. 3–4 (2019): 1–11; Spencer, "Understanding the Mentoring Process between Adolescents and Adults."

24. N. Deutsch and R. Spencer, "Capturing the Magic: Assessing the Quality of Youth Mentoring Relationships," *New Directions in Youth Development: Theory, Practice and Research* 121 (2009): 47–70; Keller and Pryce, "Mutual but Unequal"; N. R. Thomson and D. H. Zand, "Mentees' Perceptions of Their Interpersonal Relationships: The Role of the Mentor-Youth Bond," *Youth Society* 41 (2010): 434–445.

25. B. E. Wampold, "How Important Are the Common Factors in Psychotherapy?: An Update," *World Psychiatry* 14, no. 3 (2015): 273.

26. R. Elliott et al., "Empathy," in *Psychotherapy Relationships That Work* (New York: Oxford University Press, 2011), 132–152.

27. D. W. Sue, P. Arredondo, and R. J. McDavis, "Multicultural Counseling Competencies and Standards: A Call to the Profession," *Journal of Multicultural Counseling and Development* 20, no. 2 (1992): 64–88.

28. J. N. Hook et al., *Cultural Humility: Engaging Diverse Identities in Therapy* (Washington, DC: American Psychological Association, 2017).

29. C. Suárez-Orozco et al., "An Integrative Risk and Resilience Model for Understanding the Adaptation of Immigrant-Origin Children and Youth," *American Psychologist* 73, no. 6 (2018): 781.

30. C. Suárez-Orozco et al., "An Integrative Risk and Resilience Model for Understanding the Adaptation of Immigrant-Origin Children and Youth."

31. B. D. McLeod, "Relation of the Alliance with Outcomes in Youth Psychotherapy: A Meta-analysis," *Clinical Psychology Review* 31,

no. 4 (2011): 603–616; S. R. Shirk, M. S. Karver, and R. Brown, "The Alliance in Child and Adolescent Psychotherapy," *Psychotherapy* 48, no. 1 (2011): 17.

32. R. Spencer, "'It's Not What I Expected': Mentoring Relationship Failures," *Journal of Adolescent Research* 22, no. 4 (2007): 331–354; R. Spencer et al., "Breaking Up Is Hard to Do: A Qualitative Interview Study of How and Why Youth Mentoring Relationships End," *Youth & Society* 49, no. 4 (2017): 438–460.

33. J. R. Weisz et al., "Performance of Evidence-Based Youth Psychotherapies Compared with Usual Clinical Care: A Multilevel Meta-analysis," *JAMA Psychiatry* 70, no. 7 (2013): 750–761.

34. K. L. Philip, J. S. Shucksmith, and C. King, *Sharing a Laugh?: A Qualitative Study of Mentoring Interventions with Young People* (York, UK: Joseph Rowntree Foundation, 2004); M. B. Styles and K. V. Morrow, *Understanding How Youth and Elders Form Relationships: A Study of Four Linking Lifetimes Programs* (Philadelphia: Public / Private Ventures, 1992).

35. D. Lakind, M. Atkins, and J. M. Eddy, "Youth Mentoring Relationships in Context: Mentor Perceptions of Youth, Environment, and the Mentor Role," *Children and Youth Services Review* 53 (2015): 52–60.

36. T. E. Keller, "The Stages and Development of Mentoring Relationships," in *Handbook of Youth Mentoring*, ed. D. L. DuBois and M. J. Karcher (Thousand Oaks, CA: SAGE, 2005), 82–99; Keller and Pryce, "Mutual but Unequal."

37. McQuillin et al., "Strengthening and Expanding Child Services in Low Resource Communities."

38. D. L. DuBois et al., "Effectiveness of Mentoring Programs for Youth: A Meta-analytic Review," *American Journal of Community Psychology* 30, no. 2 (2002): 157–197; C. Herrera et al., *Making a Difference in Schools: The Big Brothers Big Sisters School-Based Mentoring Impact Study* (Philadelphia: Public / Private Ventures, 2007); A. M. Omoto and M. Snyder, "Sustained Helping without

Obligation: Motivation, Longevity of Service, and Perceived Attitude Change among AIDS Volunteers," *Journal of Personality and Social Psychology* 68, no. 4 (1995): 671; S. M. Martin and S. K. Sifers, "An Evaluation of Factors Leading to Mentor Satisfaction with the Mentoring Relationship," *Children and Youth Services Review* 34, no. 5 (2012): 940–945; S. D. McQuillin, G. G. Straight, and E. Saeki, "Program Support and Value of Training in Mentors' Satisfaction and Anticipated Continuation of School-Based Mentoring Relationships," in *Mentoring and Tutoring: Partnership in Learning* 23, no. 2 (2015): 133–148.

39. DuBois et al., "Effectiveness of Mentoring Programs for Youth."
40. J. B. Kupersmidt et al., "Predictors of Premature Match Closure in Youth Mentoring Relationships," *American Journal of Community Psychology* 59, no. 1–2 (2017): 25–35.
41. J. B. Kupersmidt et al., "Predictors of Premature Match Closure in Youth Mentoring Relationships."

8. THE ROAD TO RIGOR

1. J. R. Weisz et al., "A Proposal to Unite Two Different Worlds of Children's Mental Health," *American Psychologist* 61, no. 6 (2006): 644–645.
2. C. Herrera, D. L. DuBois, and J. B. Grossman, *The Role of Risk: Mentoring Experiences and Outcomes for Youth with Varying Risk Profiles* (New York: Public / Private Ventures, 2013).
3. R. Putnam, *Our Kids: The American Dream in Crisis* (New York: Simon and Schuster, 2015).
4. P. J. Jones et al., "An Upper Limit to Youth Psychotherapy Benefit?: A Meta-analytic Copula Approach to Psychotherapy Outcomes," *Clinical Psychological Science* 7, no. 6 (2019): 1434–1449.
5. A. Giridharadas, *Winners Take All: The Elite Charade of Changing the World* (New York: Knopf, 2018).
6. G. Walker, *Mentoring, Policy, and Politics* (Philadelphia: Public / Private Ventures, 2007), 522.

7. James J. Heckman, "Invest in Early Childhood Development: Reduce Deficits, Strengthen the Economy," Heckman Equation, 2012, https://heckmanequation.org/www/assets/2013/07/F _HeckmanDeficitPieceCUSTOM-Generic_052714-3-1.pdf.

8. T. Weiston-Serdon, *Critical Mentoring: A Practical Guide* (Herndon, VA: Stylus, 2017); J. N. Albright, N. M. Hurd, and S. B. Hussain, "Applying a Social Justice Lens to Youth Mentoring: A Review of the Literature and Recommendations for Practice," *American Journal of Community Psychology* 59, no. 3–4 (2017): 363–381.

9. B. A. Stevenson, "Commencement Address," College of the Holy Cross, 2015, https://www.holycross.edu/commencement /commencement-archives/commencement-2015/stevenson -address.

10. Margaret Mead, "On Being a Grandmother," in *Development through Life: A Case Study Approach,* ed. B. M. Newman and P. R. Newman (Homewood, IL: Dorsey, 1972), 293–300.

9. WHY WE CAN'T LEAVE NATURAL MENTORING TO CHANCE

1. M. Bruce and J. Bridgeland, *The Mentoring Effect: Young People's Perspectives on the Outcomes and Availability of Mentoring* (Washington, DC: MENTOR, 2014); E. B. Raposa et al., "How Economic Disadvantage Affects the Availability and Nature of Mentoring Relationships during the Transition to Adulthood," *American Journal of Community Psychology* 61, no. 1–2 (2018): 191–203; D. L. DuBois and N. Silverthorn, "Characteristics of Natural Mentoring Relationships and Adolescent Adjustment: Evidence from a National Study," *Journal of Primary Prevention* 26, no. 2 (2005): 69–92.

2. R. Putnam, *Our Kids: The American Dream in Crisis* (New York: Simon and Schuster, 2015).

3. Putnam, *Our Kids.*

4. K. M. Harris et al., "The National Longitudinal Study of Adolescent Health: Research Design," Add Health, 2003, http://www.cpc .unc.edu/projects/addhealth/design.

5. M. A. Hagler and J. E. Rhodes, "The Long-Term Impact of Natural Mentoring Relationships: A Counterfactual Analysis," *American Journal of Community* Psychology 62, no. 1–2 (2018): 175–188.

6. DuBois and Silverthorn, "Characteristics of Natural Mentoring Relationships and Adolescent Adjustment"; V. M. Fruiht and L. Wray-Lake, "The Role of Mentor Type and Timing in Predicting Educational Attainment," *Journal of Youth and Adolescence* 42 (2013): 1459–1472; S. McDonald and J. Lambert, "The Long Arm of Mentoring: A Counterfactual Analysis of Natural Youth Mentoring and Employment Outcomes in Early Careers," *American Journal of Community Psychology* 54 (2014): 262–273; T. Miranda-Chan et al., "The Functions and Longitudinal Outcomes of Adolescents' Naturally Occurring Mentorships," *American Journal of Community Psychology* 57 (2016): 47–59; Raposa et al., "How Economic Disadvantage Affects the Availability and Nature of Mentoring Relationships during the Transition to Adulthood"; Z. C. Timpe and E. Lunkenheimer, "The Long-Term Economic Benefits of Natural Mentoring Relationships for Youth," *American Journal of Community Psychology* 56, no. 1–2 (2015): 12–24; McDonald and Lambert, "The Long Arm of Mentoring"; Hagler and Rhodes, "The Long-Term Impact of Natural Mentoring Relationships."

7. Gallup. "Great Jobs Great Lives: The 2014 Gallup-Purdue Index Report," Gallup.com, 2014, https://www.gallup.com/services /176768/2014-gallup-purdue-index-report.aspx.

8. J. Engle and V. Tinto, "Moving beyond Access: College Success for Low-Income, First-Generation Students," Pell Institute for the Study of Opportunity in Higher Education, 2008, http://files.eric .ed.gov/fulltext/ED504448.pdf; R. D. Stanton-Salazar, "A Social Capital Framework for the Study of Institutional Agents and Their Role in the Empowerment of Low-Status Students and Youth," *Youth & Society* 43 (2011): 1066–1109; E. S. Chang et al., "Nonparental Adults as Social Resources in the Transition to Adulthood," *Journal of Research on Adolescence* 20 (2010): 1065–1082;

D. S. Black et al., "The Influence of School-Based Natural Mentoring Relationships on School Attachment and Subsequent Adolescent Risk Behaviors," *Health Education Research* 25 (2010): 892–902; N. M. Hurd and R. M. Sellers, "Black Adolescents' Relationships with Natural Mentors: Associations with Academic Engagement via Social and Emotional Development," *Cultural Diversity and Ethnic Minority Psychology* 19 (2013): 76–85; N. Hurd and M. Zimmerman, "Natural Mentors, Mental Health, and Risk Behaviors: A Longitudinal Analysis of African American Adolescents Transitioning into Adulthood," *American Journal of Community Psychology* 46, no. 1–2 (2010): 36–48; N. M. Hurd, J. S. Tan, and E. L. Loeb, "Natural Mentoring Relationships and the Adjustment to College among Underrepresented Students," *American Journal of Community Psychology* 57 (2016): 330–341; S. M. Kogan, G. H. Brody, and Y. Chen, "Natural Mentoring Processes Deter Externalizing Problems among Rural African American Emerging Adults: A Prospective Analysis," *American Journal of Community Psychology* 48 (2011): 272–283; R. D. Stanton-Salazar and U. Spina, "Informal Mentors and Role Models in the Lives of Urban Mexican-Origin Adolescents," *Anthropology and Education Quarterly* 34, no. 3 (2003): 231–254; M. Garringer and C. Benning, *The Power of Relationships: How and Why American Adults Step Up to Mentor the Nation's Youth* (Boston: MENTOR, 2018).

9. L. Van Dam et al., "Does Natural Mentoring Matter?: A Multilevel Meta-analysis on the Association between Natural Mentoring and Youth Outcomes," *American Journal of Community Psychology* 62 (2017): 203–220.

10. Van Dam et al., "Does Natural Mentoring Matter?"

11. Bruce and Bridgeland, *The Mentoring Effect*; Hagler and Rhodes, "The Long-Term Impact of Natural Mentoring Relationships"; Putnam, *Our Kids.*

12. R. Chetty et al., "Race and Economic Opportunity in the United States: An Intergenerational Perspective," NBER Working Papers

Series, no. 24441 (Cambridge, MA: National Bureau of Economic Research, 2018); S. F. Reardon and K. Bischoff, "Income Inequality and Income Segregation," *American Journal of Sociology* 116, no. 4 (2011): 1092–1153.

13. W. J. Wilson, "Toward a Framework for Understanding Forces That Contribute to or Reinforce Racial Inequality," *Race and Social Problems* 1, no. 1 (2009): 3–11.

14. Putnam, *Our Kids.*

15. E. B. Raposa and N. M. Hurd, "Understanding Networks of Natural Mentoring Support among Underrepresented College Students," *Applied Developmental Science* 8691 (2018): 1–12.

16. N. M. Hurd et al., "Appraisal Support from Natural Mentors, Self-Worth, and Psychological Distress: Examining the Experiences of Underrepresented Students Transitioning through College," *Journal of Youth and Adolescence* 47, no. 5 (2018): 1100–1112; Raposa and Hurd, "Understanding Networks of Natural Mentoring Support among Underrepresented College Students."

17. S. Ferguson, "Ask Not What Your Mentor Can Do for You . . . : The Role of Reciprocal Exchange in Maintaining Student–Teacher Mentorships," *Sociological Forum* 33, no. 1 (March 2018): 211–233; K. R. Wentzel and A. Wigfield, "Introduction," in *Handbook of Motivation in School*, ed. K. R. Wentzel and A. Wigfield (New York: Routledge, 2009), 1–8.

18. R. C. Pianta, B. K. Hamre, and J. P. Allen, "Teacher-Student Relationships and Engagement: Conceptualizing, Measuring, and Improving the Capacity of Classroom Interactions," in *Handbook of Research on Student Engagement* (Boston: Springer, 2012), 370.

19. R. Chetty, J. N. Friedman, and J. E. Rockoff, "Measuring the Impacts of Teachers II: Teacher Value-Added and Student Outcomes in Adulthood," *American Economic Review* 104, no. 9 (2014): 2633–2679.

20. L. D. Erickson, S. McDonald, and G. H. Elder, "Informal Mentors and Education: Complementary or Compensatory Resources?,"

Sociological Education 82 (2009): 344–367; S. McDonald et al., "Informal Mentoring and Young Adult Employment," *Social Science Research* 36 (2007): 1328–1347.

21. Stanton-Salazar and Spina, "Informal Mentors and Role Models in the Lives of Urban Mexican-Origin Adolescents"; V. Tinto, *Leaving College: Rethinking the Causes and Cures of Student Attrition* (Chicago: University of Chicago Press, 1987).

22. K. M. Christensen et al., "The Role of Athletic Coach Mentors in Promoting Youth Academic Success: Evidence from the Add Health National Longitudinal Study," *Applied Developmental Science* no. 23 (2019): 1–11; Raposa et al., "How Economic Disadvantage Affects the Availability and Nature of Mentoring Relationships during the Transition to Adulthood"; Hagler and Rhodes, "The Long-Term Impact of Natural Mentoring Relationships."

23. Hagler and Rhodes, "The Long-Term Impact of Natural Mentoring Relationships."

24. Hagler and Rhodes, "The Long-Term Impact of Natural Mentoring Relationships."

25. R. Crosnoe, K. Monica, and H. Glen, "School Size and the Interpersonal Side of Education: An Examination of Race / Ethnicity and Organizational Context," *Social Sciences Quarterly* 85 (2004): 1259–1274; Erickson, McDonald, and Elder, "Informal Mentors and Education"; J. R. Ancis, W. E. Sedlacek, and J. J. Mohr, "Student Perceptions of Campus Cultural Climate by Race," *Journal of Counseling and Development* 78, no. 2 (2000): 180–185; C. Murray and K. M. Murray, "Child Level Correlates of Teacher–Student Relationships: An Examination of Demographic Characteristics, Academic Orientations, and Behavioral Orientations," *Psychology in the Schools* 41, no. 7 (2004): 751–762.

26. A. A. Jack, "(No) Harm in Asking: Class, Acquired Cultural Capital, and Academic Engagement at an Elite University," *Sociology of Education* 89, no. 1 (2016): 1–19; A. Lareau, "Cultural Knowledge and Social Inequality," *American Sociological Review* 80,

no. 1 (2015): 1–27; J. M. Calarco, "'I Need help!' Social Class and Children's Help-Seeking in Elementary School," *American Sociological Review* 76, no. 6 (2011): 862–882; J. M. Calarco, "The Inconsistent Curriculum: Cultural Tool Kits and Student Interpretations of Ambiguous Expectations," *Social Psychology Quarterly* 77, no. 2 (2014): 185–209.

27. Ferguson, "Ask Not What Your Mentor Can Do for You . . ."

28. J. N. Jones and N. L. Deutsch, "Relational Strategies in After-School Settings: How Staff-Youth Relationships Support Positive Development," *Youth & Society* 43 (2011): 1381–1406; J. E. Rhodes, "A Model of Youth Mentoring," in *Handbook of Youth Mentoring*, ed. D. L. DuBois and M. J. Karcher (Thousand Oaks, CA: SAGE, 2005), 30–43, http://ir.obihiro.ac.jp/dspace/handle/10322/3933; R. O. Rubin et al., "Striking a Balance: An Exploration of Staff-Camper Relationship Formation," *Journal of Youth Development* 13 (2018): 44–61.

29. M. W. McLaughlin, *You Can't Be What You Can't See: The Power of Opportunity to Change Young Lives* (Cambridge, MA: Harvard Education Press, 2018).

30. B. J. Hirsch and V. Wong, "After-School Programs," in *Handbook of Youth Mentoring*, 364–375.

31. E. Choi et al., "The Influence of a Sports Mentoring Program on Children's Life Skills Development," *Journal of Physical Education and Sport* 15, no. 2 (2015): 264; M. D. Hoffmann and T. M. Loughead, "A Comparison of Well-Peer Mentored and Non-peer Mentored Athletes' Perceptions of Satisfaction," *Journal of Sports Sciences* 34, no. 5 (2016): 450–458.

32. Christensen et al., "The Role of Athletic Coach Mentors in Promoting Youth Academic Success."

33. M. S. Granovetter, "The Strength of Weak Ties," *American Journal of Sociology* 78 (1978): 1360–1380.

34. A. Lareau, *Unequal Childhoods: Class, Race and Family Life* (Berkeley: University of California Press, 2003); Putnam, *Our Kids.*

35. Stanton-Salazar, "A Social Capital Framework for the Study of Institutional Agents and Their Role in the Empowerment of Low-Status Students and Youth"; Stanton-Salazar and Spina, "Informal Mentors and Role Models in the Lives of Urban Mexican-Origin Adolescents."

36. Hagler and Rhodes, "The Long-Term Impact of Natural Mentoring Relationships."

37. E. C. Roehlkepartain et al., *Relationships First: Creating Connections That Help Young People Thrive* (Minneapolis: Search Institute, 2017).

38. J. N. Hughes and T. A. Cavell, "Influence of the Teacher-Student Relationship in Childhood Conduct Problems: A Prospective Study," *Journal of Clinical Child Psychology* 28, no. 2 (1999): 173.

39. J. Reynolds and M. Parrish, "Natural Mentors, Social Class, and College Success," *American Journal of Community Psychology* 61 (2018): 179–190.

40. M. Ashtinai and C. Feliciano, *Low-Income Young Adults Continue to Face Barriers to College Entry and Degree Completion: Research Brief,* Pathways to Postsecondary Success, All Campus Consortium on Research for Diversity, 2012, https://pathways.gseis.ucla.edu /publications/201201_ashtianifelicianoRB_online.pdf; Erickson, McDonald, and Elder, "Informal Mentors and Education"; Fruiht and Wray-Lake, "The Role of Mentor Type and Timing in Predicting Educational Attainment"; Timpe and Lunkenheimer, "The Long-Term Economic Benefits of Natural Mentoring Relationships for Youth"; V. Fruiht and T. Chan, "Naturally Occurring Mentorship in a National Sample of First-Generation College Goers: A Promising Portal for Academic and Developmental Success," *American Journal of Community Psychology* 61, no. 3–4 (2018): 386–397.

41. K. L. Milkman, M. Akinola, and D. Chugh, "What Happens Before?: A Field Experiment Exploring How Pay and Representation Differentially Shape Bias on the Pathway into Organizations," *Journal of Applied Psychology* 100 (2015): 1678–1712.

42. L. A. Rivera and A. Tilcsik, "Class Advantage, Commitment Penalty: The Gendered Effect of Social Class Signals in an Elite Labor Market," *American Sociological Review* 81, no. 6 (2016): 1097–1131.

43. "Missed Opportunities: The Labor Market in Health Informatics, 2014," Burning Glass, 2018, https://www.burning-glass.com /research-project/health-informatics-2014/.

44. G. Ward and D. Keltner, "Power and the Consumption of Resources" (unpublished manuscript, 1998) as cited in "The Experience of Power: Examining the Effects of Power on Approach and Inhibition Tendencies" by C. Anderson and J. Berdahl, *Journal of Personality and Social Psychology* 83, no. 6 (2003): 1362–1377.

45. J. Kottke, "Michael Lewis and the Parable of the Lucky Man Taking the Extra Cookie," 2017, https://kottke.org/17/06/michael -lewis-and-the-parable-of-the-lucky-man-taking-the-extra-cookie.

46. M. Lewis, "Princeton University's 2012 Baccalaureate Remarks," 2012, https://www.princeton.edu/news/2012/06/03/princeton -universitys-2012-baccalaureate-remarks.

47. M. Millenky, "Connecting High School Dropouts to Employment and Education: An Impact Study of the National Guard Youth Challenge Program," *IZA Journal of Labor Policy* 5, no. 10 (2016): 1–17.

48. S. E. Schwartz et al., "'I'm Having a Little Struggle with This, Can You Help Me Out?': Examining Impacts and Processes of a Social Capital Intervention for First-Generation College Students," *American Journal of Community Psychology* 61, no. 1–2 (2018): 166–178.

49. Hurd et al., "Appraisal Support from Natural Mentors, Self-Worth, and Psychological Distress"; J. K. Greeson and A. E. Thompson, "Development, Feasibility, and Piloting of a Novel Natural Mentoring Intervention for Older Youth in Foster Care," *Journal of Social Service Research* 43, no. 2 (2017): 205–222; L. Van Dam et al., "Does Natural Mentoring Matter?: A Multilevel Meta-analysis on the Association between Natural Mentoring and

Youth Outcomes," *American Journal of Community Psychology* 62, no. 1–2 (2018): 203–220.

50. C. A. King et al., "Association of the Youth-Nominated Support Team Intervention for Suicidal Adolescents with 11- to 14-Year Mortality Outcomes: Secondary Analysis of a Randomized Clinical Trial," *JAMA Psychiatry* 6, no. 5 (2019): 492–498.

51. K. Pekel et al., "Finding the Fluoride: Examining How and Why Developmental Relationships Are the Active Ingredient in Interventions That Work," *American Journal of Orthopsychiatry* 88, no. 5 (2018): 493–502.

52. M. Freedman, *How to Live Forever: The Enduring Power of Connecting the Generations* (New York: PublicAffairs, 2018); P. Uhlenberg and J. De Jong Gierveld, "Age-Segregation in Later Life: An Examination of Personal Networks," *Ageing and Society* 24, no. 1 (2004): 5–28.

53. Freedman, *How to Live Forever.*

10. THE FUTURE OF MENTORING

1. R. S. Baker and K. Yacef, "The State of Educational Data Mining in 2009: A Review and Future Visions," *Journal of Educational Data Mining* 1, no. 1 (2009): 3–17.

2. T. Baker, R. McFall, and V. Shoham, "Is Your Therapist a Little Behind the Times?," *Washington Post,* November 16, 2009.

3. J. D. Frank and J. Frank, *Persuasion and Healing: A Comparative Study of Psychotherapy* (Baltimore: Johns Hopkins University Press, 1973).

4. M. J. Karcher, *The Cross-Age Mentoring Program (CAMP) for Children with Adolescent Mentors: Program Manual* (San Antonio, TX: Developmental Press, 2012); M. J. Karcher and M. J. Nakkula, "Youth Mentoring with a Balanced Focus, Shared Purpose, and Collaborative Interactions," *New Directions in Youth Development* 126 (Summer 2010): 13–32.

5. T. M. Veludo-de-Oliveira, J. G. Pallister, and G. R. Foxall, "Unselfish?: Understanding the Role of Altruism, Empathy, and

Beliefs in Volunteering Commitment," *Journal of Nonprofit and Public Sector Marketing* 27, no. 4 (2015): 373-396.

EPILOGUE

1. Homer, *The Odyssey* (London, New York: G. P. Putnam's Sons, 1919).
2. A. Roberts, "Homer's Mentor Duties Fulfilled or Misconstrued," *History of Education Journal* 64 (1999): 81-90.
3. F. de Fénelon, *Telemachus, Son of Ulysses* (Cambridge: Cambridge University Press, 1699); Roberts, "Homer's Mentor Duties Fulfilled or Misconstrued."
4. Roberts, "Homer's Mentor Duties Fulfilled or Misconstrued."

Acknowledgments

I didn't set out to so deeply challenge the very field that I had spent decades helping to build. But midway through, when I had written myself into a corner, I realized that the only way out was through. My husband, Dane Wittrup, gave me the courage, audience, insights, and support to do so, as did my sister, Nancy McNamara. Several of my talented graduate students, especially Matt Hagler, Kirsten Christensen, Justin Preston, and Cy Poon, were instrumental in this process, answering my relentless requests with patience and rigor. MENTOR: The National Mentoring Partnership provided generous support for this work, as did the MacArthur Foundation and the William T. Grant Foundation. I am also deeply grateful to Big Brothers Big Sisters of America, whose senior leadership team received my analysis and suggestions with an unflinching commitment to improvement. Skillful editors and graphic designers, including Martha Mangelsdorf, Jessica Cohen, Max Harness, Andrew Kinney, Ron Nowak, and Hillary Sigale, helped to polish rough edges and bring structure to a messy process. I appreciate Michael Karcher, Liz Raposa, Juliet Schor, Sarah Schwartz, Renée Spencer, Carola Suarez-Orozco, Mary Waters, Niobe Way, Tim Cavell, Mike

Garringer, Stella Kanchewa, and Richard Lerner for their generous feedback and support. Finally, I am deeply grateful to my children, Audrey, Ian, and Thomas, who instruct me every day in the joys and complexities of intergenerational relationships, and without whom this book would have been completed several years ago.

INDEX

Page numbers in italics refer to tables and figures.

accountability, supportive, 106-109
Across Ages, 34
ADHD, 49
adult support, 53, 111, 129
Aftercare in Indiana through Mentoring (AIM), 99
after-school programs, and natural mentoring, 134-135
Albee, George, 71, 151
alliance, working, 111-112, 113-116, 117-119. *See also* relationship-building; therapeutic relationships
apps, smartphone, 102-109
Arches Transformative Mentoring program, 87-88
Aronson, Elliot, 66
arts programs, and natural mentoring, 134-135
athletic programs and coaches, 52, 134-136
attrition, 53-56, 89-90, 92-93
authenticity, 115, 117
Les aventures de Telemaque (Fénelon), 149-151
adverse childhood experiences, 4

Baker, David, 24
Becoming a Man (BAM), 69
behavioral problems, 4, 34, 49, 51, 55, 91-92
behavioral regulation skills, 73-74, 91-92, 94, 101
"benevolent dolphin, problem of," 66
biases, 62-67, 138-139, 144
Big Brothers and Big Sisters: genesis of, 3, 9-11; merges with juvenile court reform movement, 12; becomes national organization, 12-13; as compassion-driven, 13-14; impact studies on, 19-20; return-on-investment studies on, 33; attrition rates in, 53-54
Biglan, Anthony, 91
black families: Progressivism and, 14-15; comfort with youth mentoring programs, 50-51
blended mentoring programs, 85, 102-109, 145
Bloom, Paul, 63
bonds, lasting, 89-90
Bornstein, Daniel, 98
Boys and Girls Clubs, 135

Brooks, David, 53–54
burnout, 53–56, 89–90, 92–93

Cambridge-Somerville Youth Study, 19, 20, 41
caregivers, relationship between mentors and, 116–120
Cavell, Tim, 87, 89
chronic stress, 100–101
City Connects, 100
class: and natural mentoring, 130, 132–138; and bias against marginalized youth, 138–139; and privilege, 139–141. *See also* poverty
cognitive-behavioral therapy principles, 73, 87–88, 91, 99, 104, 115
cognitive biases, 62–67, 138–139, 144
college attendance, and evidence-based approaches in youth interventions, 112
"common factors," 109, 111, 145
community schools, and embedded mentoring, 99–100
compassion, 13–14, 63. *See also* empathy
Connected Scholars, 141–142
connection, bids for, 110–111
Cooley, Charles Horton, 114
cost-benefit analyses, 32–35
Coulter, Ernest Kent, 11–12, 13–14
Cross-Age Mentoring Program (CAMP), 88
cultural deprivation, negative effects of, 18
cultural empathy and humility, 115–116

Davies, William, 68
DiVittorio, Anthony, 69
"dolphin, problem of the benevolent," 66
DuBois, David, 31–32, 91
Durlak, Joseph, 74–77, 79

educational attainment, mentors' impact on, 131, 137–138
effectiveness of youth mentoring programs, 25–26; program evaluations, 27–30; meta-analysis, 30–32, *33*; return-on-investment (ROI) studies, 32–35; comparisons with other youth interventions, 36–38; countering resistance to evidence-based approaches, 39–42
Elements of Effective Practice (EEPM), 121
Elledge, Chris, 87, 89
embedded mentoring programs, 84, *85*, 97–102, 145
Embry, Dennis, 91
emotional regulation skills, 73–74, 126
empathy, 63–64, 115–116. *See also* compassion
employment, and bias against marginalized youth, 139
equality, 16–17. *See also* inequality
equity bias, 66–67
ethnicity-based bias, 138–139
evidence-based approaches in youth interventions, 36–38; countering resistance to, 39–42; weak or nonexistent outcomes in, 44; paraprofessional approach in, 81–82; and blended mentoring, 103–109; mentor training in, 124–125, 126; access to, 128. *See also* targeted approach to mentoring
Experience Corps, 97–98
expertise gap, 66–67

Fénelon, François, 149–151
formal mentoring, 2, 39, 56, 57–58, 60, 62–63, 73, 123–124, 130, 132, 147
Fostering Healthy Futures, 98–99
Frank, Jerome, 72
Frank, Julia, 72
Freedman, Marc, 53

friendship approach to mentoring: described, 2–3; and resistance to evidence-based approaches, 40; as insufficient, 43; and underestimation of mentee risks, 52–53; move to "mentoring-as-context" model from, 87. *See also* nonspecific approach to mentoring
future of mentoring, 144–147

Gallup-Purdue Index survey, 131
Gardner, John, 97–98
gender-based bias, 138–139
generosity, 63
genuineness, 115, 117
Gottman, John, 111

helping backgrounds, mentors with, 80–81
high school students, as mentors, 23
Hirsch, Bart, 135
humility, cultural, 115–116

identified victim effect, 62–65
immigrants, Progressivism and, 14–15
income: school mentors' impact on, 137–138; and bias against marginalized youth, 139
income inequality, 17, 141
income segregation, 132–133, 141
inequality, 8, 15, 16–17, 25, 51, 125–126, 138–141
informal mentoring. *See* natural mentoring; youth-initiated mentoring (YIM) approaches
interventions: comparisons of youth mentoring programs and other, 36–38; as contexts for mentoring, 93–94; technology-delivered, 102–109; calibrating risk to approach to, 124; mentor support for, 124–128. *See also* evidence-based approaches in youth interventions

January, Alicia, 101
Jones, Payton, 125
Journal of Primary Prevention, 151
Julian, Megan M., 39
juvenile court reform movement, 12, 15
juvenile justice system, and embedded mentoring, 99
Juvenile Mentoring Program (JUMP), 20–21

Karcher, Michael, 52
Karlsruher, Averil, 77
Karver, Marc, 116
Keller, Thomas, 91

labor movement, 16
Lepore, Jill, 16
Lewis, Michael, 139–141
Li, Junlei, 39
life circumstances, of mentees, 47–49
"looking-glass" self, 114
Lyons, Michael, 61

Maguire, Colleen, 24
McCord, Joan, 19–20
McQuillin, Sam, 61, 90
Mead, George Herbert, 114
Mead, Margaret, 127–128
meditation apps, 105
mental health: evidence-based treatment models, 36–38; and procurement of mentoring services, 49, 51; and academic, social, and career difficulties, 73–74; paraprofessionals' impact on, 78–79, 82; and modular approach to youth mentoring, 91–92; prioritizing, 123; shifting tasks to mentors, 123–124, 146. *See also* paraprofessionals; psychotherapy

mental health apps (MHapps), 103–109
mentee risks, underestimation of, 46–56
mentees, resistance from, 113–114
Mentor (fictional character), 148–150
mentor attrition, 53–56, 89–90, 92–93
MENTOR: The National Mentoring
  Partnership, 21, 121
mentoring-as-context programs,
  87–88
Mentoring Children of Prisoners
  program, 22
mentors: personal benefits to, 83;
  training of, 90–91, 108, 120–121,
  124–125; and interventions as contexts
  for mentoring, 93–94; sensitivity and
  attunement of, 109, 110–111; impact of
  positive appraisals of, 114–115;
  authenticity of, 115, 117; relationship
  between caregivers and, 116–120;
  shifting professional mental health
  tasks to, 123–124, 146; role of, as
  supporting interventions, 124–128;
  lack of, 129; opportunities for
  becoming, 142–143; etymology of
  term, 148–150

meta-analysis, 30–32, 33
Milkman, Katherine, 138
Miller, George, 71–72
mindfulness apps, 105
miscommunication, 62–67
mistrust, 117
moderately close relationships,
  effectiveness of, 112–121, 126–128
modular approach to youth mentoring,
  91–92

National Guard Youth Challenge
  Program, 99, 141
National Implementation Research
  Network (NIRN), 90

National Longitudinal Study of
  Adolescent to Adult Health (Add
  Health), 130–131, 134
National Mentoring Resource Center, 121
natural mentoring, 58–59, 129–141. See
  also youth-initiated mentoring (YIM)
  approaches
needs, making known, 110–111
neighborhood disadvantages, 132–133
nonspecific approach to mentoring:
  described, 2–3; program evaluations,
  28, 29, 30; return-on-investment (ROI)
  analyses, 35; as most common
  approach, 38; and resistance to
  evidence-based approaches, 40;
  long-term effects of, 41; as insufficient, 42, 43; move to "mentoring-as-
  context" model from, 87. See also
  friendship approach to mentoring;
  weak or nonexistent outcomes
nonvolunteer school-based mentoring
  programs, 35

Odyssey, The (Homer), 148–149, 150
One to One Partnership, 21. See also
  MENTOR: The National Mentoring
  Partnership

Packer, George, 17
paraprofessionals, 71–72; youth
  mentoring programs and, 72–74;
  scholarship on, 74–78; effectiveness
  of, 76–79; implications for, approach
  in mentoring, 79–84; shifting
  professional mental health tasks to,
  123–124, 146
parents, relationship between mentors
  and, 116–120
positive youth development (PYD),
  56–62
poverty, 8, 18, 125. See also class

practice sessions, supervised, 94–96
Presidents' Summit for America's Future, 21
prevention science, 57, 90, 121, 122–128
privilege, 139–141
"problem of the benevolent dolphin," 66
Progressivism, 14–17
PsyberGuide.org, 108
psychotherapy, 37, 38, 39, 125. *See also* mental health; paraprofessionals
Public/Private Ventures study, 19, 20
Putnam, Robert, 130

rejection, 114
relationship-building, 39–40, 42, 89–90, 109. *See also* friendship approach to mentoring; nonspecific approach to mentoring; therapeutic relationships
researcher-practitioner communication gaps, 67–70
resistance, from mentees, 113–114
resource accessibility, awareness of, 101
retired adults, as mentors, 142–143
return-on-investment (ROI) studies, 32–35
Rivera, Lauren, 139
Roberts, Andy, 149–150
Rockefeller, John D., 16
Roosevelt, Theodore, 16

"sage/counseling" approach, 113
Schelling, Thomas, 63
school-based mentoring programs, 35
schools, paraprofessionals in, 82–83
school staff, as natural mentors, 133–134
Sechrest, Lee, 43
self-esteem and self-worth, 114
settlement houses, 15
skills development, 4–5, 113
smartphone apps, 102–109
social capital, 136

social-emotional learning programs, 100–101
specialized mentoring programs, 84, *85,* 87–96, 145
Spencer, Renée, 55, 109
Sponsor-a-Scholar, 34
sports programs, 52, 134–136
stepped-care model of supervision, 82–83
Stevenson, Bryan A., 127
storytelling, 62–65
stress, chronic, 100–101
strong ties, 136
Student Mentoring Program, 22
success stories, isolated, 62–65
summer camps, and natural mentoring, 134–135
SuperBetter, 105
supportive accountability, 106–109

targeted approach to mentoring: described, 3–5; program evaluations, 28, *29,* 30; effectiveness of, 36–38; countering resistance to, 39–42; paraprofessional approach in, 81–82; and embedded mentoring, 97–98. *See also* evidence-based approaches in youth interventions
Tavris, Carol, 66
teachers, as natural mentors, 133–134
technology-delivered interventions, 102–109
therapeutic helping relationships, effectiveness of, 36
therapeutic mentoring models, 99
therapeutic relationships: factors common to effective, 110–112; effectiveness of moderately close, 112–121, 126–128. *See also* relationship-building
therapist genuineness, 115
Thread, 98

ties, lasting, 89–90
Tilcsik, András, 139
Tobin, Vera, 64
Tolan, Patrick, 60–61
training, for volunteer mentors, 90–91, 108, 120–121, 124–125
trauma-informed cognitive-behavioral therapy, 99
treatment and prevention science, 57, 122–128
trust, earning, 118. *See also* mistrust

underemployment, 139
universal primary prevention programs, 46–47, 50–51
usual-care intervention models, 37

volunteer attrition, 53–56, 89–90, 92–93
volunteerism, 16
volunteers. *See* mentors

Walker, Gary, 126
Washington State Institute for Public Policy, 33, 34
weak or nonexistent outcomes, 43–46; and underestimation of mentee risks, 46–56; and misalignment with field of positive youth development, 56–62; and cognitive biases, 62–67; and researcher-practitioner communication gaps, 67–70
weak ties, 136
wealth gap, 17. *See also* class; inequality; poverty
Weisz, John, 37–38, 76, 119, 122–123
Westheimer, Irv, 9–11
Wheeler, Marc, 91

Wilson, William Julius, 132–133
working alliance, 111–112, 113–116, 117–119. *See also* relationship-building; therapeutic relationships
Working on Womanhood (WOW), 69

youth-initiated mentoring (YIM) approaches, 129–130, 141–143, 145. *See also* natural mentoring
youth mentoring programs: statistics concerning, 2; approaches in, 2–5, 84–86; expansion of, 5, 13, 21–24; genesis of, 9–12; Progressivism and, 14–17; second wave of, 17–20, 24; impact of, 19–20, 22, 23; domestic versus international, 25–26; school-based, 35; as universal primary prevention interventions, 46–47, 50–51; demographics concerning, 47–49; black caregivers' comfort with, 50–51; misalignment of positive youth development and, 56–62; research on, 60–62, 65, 67–69; implementation of, 61–62; and paraprofessionals, 72–74, 79–84; embedded, 84, *85*, 97–102, 145; specialized, 84, *85*, 87–96, 145; blended, 85, 102–109, 145; modular approach in, 91–92; and treatment and prevention science, 122–128; future of, 144–147. *See also* Big Brothers and Big Sisters; effectiveness of youth mentoring programs; evidence-based approaches in youth interventions; friendship approach to mentoring; nonspecific approach to mentoring; targeted approach to mentoring; weak or nonexistent outcomes
youth psychotherapy, 37, 38, 39, 125. *See also* mental health; paraprofessionals